The Christian Mother

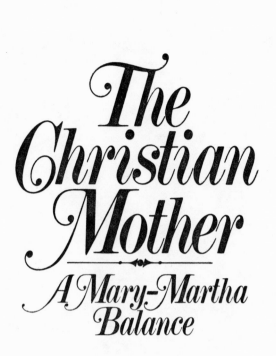

The Christian Mother

A Mary-Martha Balance

Jacky Hertz

HAWTHORN BOOKS, INC.
Publishers/ NEW YORK

THE CHRISTIAN MOTHER

Library of Congress Catalog Card Number: 76-15427
ISBN: 0-8015-1280-8
1 2 3 4 5 6 7 8 9 10

To my husband Bill and our children: Tom, Janice, Bonnie, Larry, Brian, Peggy, Bobbi, Darryl, Lolly, Mark, Vickie, Ted, and Robin. Each in his/her unique way has helped me immeasurably to reach toward my own Mary-Martha balance.

Contents

Foreword

Though at times this book may seem at odds with today's feminist thinking, it really is not. The feminist writers again and again urge us to believe in ourselves, and real liberation is our free choice of how we shall live in full knowledge of what it shall cost us and reward us.

At the base of every mature, adult life lies a necessary foundation of minute self-examination and evaluation. For the Christian woman it must be carried even further, for her values are not hers alone, but Christ's.

Most of us owe our personal evaluations today to the feminist thinkers and writers who have prodded us, however critical some of them seem of marriage and motherhood. We owe them a debt of gratitude for opening our minds to ourselves. Only by seeing the whole can we complete the self-analysis which helps us achieve the objectivity we need to pursue with joy and certainty of purpose the life-style we have chosen.

Being a wife and mother is an emotional business and without such outside urging I know I might never have seen it in perspective. But it's only through accepting and evaluating ourselves and our way of life that we grow.

The criticism that stable marriage, homemaking, and

motherhood are inhibiting to woman's true value has, for me, caused the vocation of making a home and loving a family to rise until they stand high in bold relief from the marketplace trivia which surround them like the shadows around a cameo. Here—in the Christian home—are the people, the love, and the warm life of real fulfillment.

Acknowledgments

More than to any other source, of course, I owe to Sacred Scripture my deepest gratitude for its wealth of inspiration. Without its stimulation I should never have had the courage to offer this account of our family's growth in spirituality and maturity in spite of the weaknesses and problems of its members. Scripture quotations used throughout the book are from *The Common Bible*, the *Revised Standard Version Bible*, copyright © 1973.

Grateful acknowledgment is made to the following publishers for permission to reprint articles of mine originally appearing in their publications:

Abbey Press, St. Meinrad, Indiana, for "God and the Nervous Mother."

American Baby, New York, for "You Can't Fool A Baby."

National Parent-Teacher, Chicago, Illinois, for "What 'Special Children' Can Teach Your Child."

Our Sunday Visitor, Huntington, Indiana, for "Real Love Is Discipline."

Sign, Union City, New Jersey, for "Everyone Is Important in a Family Council" and "Through Unclouded Eyes."

Acknowledgments

St. Joseph Magazine, St. Benedict, Oregon, for "Do You
Control Your TV Set or Does It Control You?,"
and "Prejudice Is Emotion—Love Is Action."
Much appreciation is owed the pastors who have unstint-
ingly given of time and self to guide our family's spiritual
lives and put up with us as we have taken two steps forward
only to take one step back.

To Geraldine Hertz, my identical twin and professional
colleague, whose Christian family life has been such an inspiration to me, and whose critical help deserves so many
thanks.

A debt of appreciation, too, to the Spokane Writers,
whose professional assistance has aided me in the writing of
this book.

The Christian Mother

1
Meet Mary and Martha

Now as they went on their way, he entered a village; and a woman named Martha received him into her house. And she had a sister called Mary, who sat at the Lord's feet and listened to his teaching. But Martha was distracted about much serving; and she went to him and said, "Lord, do you not care that my sister has left me to serve alone? Tell her then to help me." But the Lord answered her, "Martha, Martha, you are anxious and troubled about many things; one thing is needful. Mary has chosen the good portion, which shall not be taken away from her" [Luke 10:38–42].

I must confess that the last two sentences for years stopped me cold. I simply could not fathom our Lord saying *Mary* had chosen the good portion, when I visualized her as a slothful dreamer. To me she seemed not to care about a few specks of dust on the sill. Or whether the food for their guests was well done, on time, or even served hot or cold. *She* had more important things to think about than food or whether or not her dress had an unmended rip in the hem. She was lost in a contemplative fog that filled her mind and soul.

On the other hand, I thought of the bustling Martha as plump and immaculate, her hair drawn back severely from cheeks rosy with heat from the oven. Surely *she* would never tolerate dust, yet she lived in a desert country filled with it. She was so hospitable she always kept plenty of well-cooked food on reserve for company that was free to stop by. Her home was her first love.

Like Martha, during my first years of marriage, when I became plagued with dust and duties as she was, it was the image of the seemingly slothful Mary that dangled so tantalizingly before me whenever I became swamped with dishes, diapers, and plugged drains. And again I would get exasperated, especially since Jesus not only had condoned Mary's conduct but had even rebuked Martha, however gently.

Why, I thought more than once, households all across the country would fall apart if every woman took his words at their face value and simply dropped to her knees to pray and meditate on him, while she left the housework undone. For one thing, *I* had no Martha to pick up after me or my family. But then I'd think about the two sisters again and how Mary, even later when their brother Lazarus died and she heard Jesus was coming, took a dear friend's arrival far too casually. She simply stayed at home and waited patiently, while *Martha* rushed first to the edge of town to meet him and say: "Lord, if you had been here, my brother would not have died. And even now I know that whatever you ask from God, God will give you." Jesus said to her, "Your brother will rise again." Martha must have looked puzzled as she replied, only half understanding,

> "I know he will rise again in the resurrection at the last day." Jesus said to her, "I am the resurrection and the life; he who believes in me, though he die, yet shall he live, and whoever lives and believes in me shall never die. Do you believe this?" She said to him, "Yes Lord; I believe that you are the Christ, the Son of God, he who is coming into the world" [John 11:21-28].

But there must have been annoyance and envy in her

heart, too, as she went back home to whisper to her sister Mary, "The Teacher is here and is calling for you' " (John 11:28). She must have been as irritated as I often get when overwrought with responsibility, especially when I fall short, as Martha was, of understanding the real depth of love that Jesus was offering her. Slowly I began to understand that maybe Martha had been trying too hard, and that in so doing she made of her home a shrine before which all else took second place—even God. There is a world of difference between *understanding* the words of faith—the facts—and knowing our Lord intimately. Martha, it seems to me, failed to understand because she was too absorbed in her housework, whereas Mary sounded the depths of that love, though she seemed so slothful. This, remember, was the Mary who anointed the Lord with perfume and dried his feet with her hair. (John 11:2) Some believe she may have been Mary Magdalene.

Whoever she was, Mary had a secret. Somewhere, somehow, I puzzled, there must be an important reason that Jesus said Mary had chosen the better portion while he was equally willing to partake of Martha's food and hospitality.

Martha strongly resembles the woman everyone used to expect young girls to become after they grew up and married. I was no exception. Bill and I married in 1939 and I began life within a framework of the respected Martha. But as I found my way of life making me less my own woman, less the mother I wanted to be, I slowly and with great difficulty broke through the "accepted" bonds of the ages which, I now believe, is what Jesus must have intended that day so long ago. For a life of unadulterated housework, I knew, was making me less the woman I felt God wanted me to be.

The family problems dealt with in this book have always been brought about by my failing to see or once more losing the balance that God always and constantly offers to mothers. My mind changes slowly and I've had to be led to, forced to, face up to my shortcomings. I was brought to the resolution of each problem, as you'll see, as I learned first to attain, then, over and over, how to regain that balance between the busy Martha and the contemplative Mary.

As a homemaker and in the years when I was a businesswoman, I have stumbled along, slowly learning how to evolve from a harried and busy Martha who loved, but not deeply enough, toward the tranquillity and peace of Mary, a tranquillity found in moments that have given my life not only balance but a depth of meaning for myself that has continued to enrich my own sense of self-worth.

Had I known when I married Bill that we'd end up with thirteen real live, mischievous, overenergetic children, I would probably have backed out. But that only shows how much more our heavenly Father knows about what we can do, how we can stretch spiritually, than the rest of us know, for we are only creatures of his. He must have smiled and considered that it would take that many little people before *I* could grasp, for good and all, the fact that I *needed* to contemplate. To lean on him, to let things go once in awhile just to sit and rest in him in undivided awareness as Mary did so long ago.

Most of us suspect even before we say our vows that marriage and motherhood at their best will *not* be a tripping to our own tunes, no matter how liberated we are. And after a few years and a child or two, we *know* this bowl of cherries has its share of stems, leaves, and pits.

It's because of these stems, leaves, and pits, which are really nothing more than the humanness and cussedness of our mortal natures, that it is a rare woman who is content to be only a Martha, a simple *hausfrau* who never looks up or out of her world of diapers and mops. Women have a basic *need* for the nearness of God.

Christian mothers easily become Marthas. In fact, most of us begin that way, until our own restlessness and dissatisfaction tell us, as mine did, that it is not enough.

On the other hand, those who begin marriage as Marys often find motherhood a drag. A jarring interference with their spiritual meditations. Yet how *can* a child be a logical interference, at odds with the true character of woman, whose nature it is to bear and love and rear it?

Only, ignoring the child, doing your own thing in this vocation of motherhood doesn't work either except occasionally. But then, I've never heard of *any* career in which an individual can do her own thing. There are disciplines and pecking orders in all businesses and for the same reason we have them in our homes—to prevent childish chaos dangerous to all concerned.

But motherhood unleavened by the spiritual goals and values of the Christian is like unleavened dough. Teary, damp, and unpleasant. A Martha mother, as I see her, is like the unrisen dough.

In all my years of marriage, I've come across but one total Martha. She and I graduated from high school in the same class and at that time she'd been attractive and fun to be around.

I think I only realized how much was lacking in unleavened motherhood when I saw her five years after we'd both married. I was excited when I met her in a department store, and looked forward to going to her apartment later for a real visit. Those two hours stand alone as the longest in my life.

This girl, who had been as involved as the rest of us at school, had sagged into a sodden human being who by this time had turned totally inward. Every time I mentioned *anything* outside of her babies, her lemon pie, or the latest cleanser, she went vacant. Thank God *she* seemed happy, because I felt very sorry for her husband and children. As I left her, I was in deep thought. She'd given me a side of motherhood that was appalling.

I've known a few total Marys, too, whose children are hungry and dirty while they commune with their respective Muses. Some are pious intellectuals whose intellect has never connected with their common sense. Others are artists of various kinds who have missed the deepest artistic pattern of all—the human persons our Lord has created in his image. In either instance, the Marys are as unattractive as the Marthas.

There needs to be a balance. Talented women whose gifts include motherhood require something more, and did even in the early forties when our first children came along. That something more is the inclusion in our lives of the Lord whose love helps us outreach our mortal cussedness so that we can become more stimulating, more fulfilled women and mothers.

In this last quarter of the twentieth century mothers are beginning to think for themselves. Now, more than at any time in history, the need for well-thought-out uses for their talents climbs, whether they work inside the home or outside. It takes intelligence, as much education as a woman can manage, and certainly the use of the God-centered wisdom that is ours for the asking, to strike a balance in our lives and maintain it through the ups and downs of this teeter-totter we call modern Christian motherhood.

Today's woman is in the process of breaking old patterns and forming new, individualistic ones, and the time has been a long while arriving.

Each one of you today can find the delicate balance to your lives of service to family and to humankind that begins and ends with your inner need for spiritual and personal fulfillment. And you can do it with more acceptance and therefore less guilt than I had during some of the rough changes in my life.

When we began our family, I was certain I'd never be able to handle more than four children without outside help. Ha! The times we've had household help have been very brief, even when we had the means, because part of a family's beauty is its private sharing.

Even then Bill and I believed parenthood was the most beautiful, enviable, and spiritually demanding part of married life. We still think so, and that includes sex.

You can imagine our shock, then, after we learned we were to have our first baby just before World War II, when one couple after another heard the news and responded with, "You're having a baby in *this* day and age? Don't you *know* babies are only cannon fodder?"

"Not for us, they're not," I said grimly. But the war in Europe made me uneasy too. Today is not so different, is it? There have *always* been those around who cut down parenthood. I think their attitude is sour grapes.

Being a mother is no jar of honey. But when our first baby came along and in the early postwar years, America was still gung ho for marital togetherness deep enough and broad enough to flatten a better woman than I. Somewhere during those early insecure years of learning how to be a mother, I stumbled across a truth so obvious it had been in my way all along. That the only way to be a better mother was to be a better person myself. And to do that, I had to learn just who I was.

Liberation, of course. Only nobody called it that. It just sort of entered into our lives without fanfare in little ways that gradually encompassed the entire family until it has not been as painful for us as for most to release our children when they grow to adulthood. With a solid start, young people far more easily make their own way.

Recently our daughter, a college junior, told me, "Mom, you have no idea how scared other parents are for their kids. And they don't trust 'em even when they're as old as I am."

"Huh?" I blinked. "Twenty-one is a little late *not* to be trusted. If I couldn't trust you even at sixteen, I'd never have been able to sleep."

"I guess. But you'll never know how glad I am *you're* so sure I'm not going to hell the first chance I get." She grinned impishly. "It's a *very* neat anchor when the going gets rough."

That her words set up little worries in my mind didn't have to unsettle her, too. After all, I never stop being a mother, even if I have learned how to reassure our kids. But my kind of women's liberation is not the kind where equal dignity between the sexes is dumped into the same sack with abortion, lesbianism, and marriages so open they fall apart at the seams.

Bill and I have learned the long way around, that a mom is as valuable as a dad and that each child equals either of us. When dad gets the lion's share here, it isn't because he's grabbed it or necessarily "deserves" it at the moment. It's just that I love him enough to give it. Period. As he still loves me enough after thirty-seven years of marriage to open doors and lift heavy loads and hold hands with me as we walk down the street.

Every woman's personal liberation, whether from a Mary or a Martha, comes slowly and painfully. In our early years, had I once in my twenty-eight-hour day had the opportunity to glance with longing at my old neglected hobbies of oil painting or music, I'd have been lucky.

I believe today that being a Christian makes finding oneself easier. Nor did I learn *that* without a long trial. I was not baptized until I was nineteen, and my parents violently opposed my choice of Catholicism. Which means I was forced to make a difficult decision onto the path I felt right for me in following Christ, even before our first baby was born. A decision that meant I'd cut the apron strings, but even after they're cut, such strings always leave trails of guilt if we let them. And I let them for a long time.

The church I chose has offered me rich graces and teachings that have helped me, a convert particularly prone to misunderstandings. I've had continually to question and consider and seek. It was only natural that this seeking seemed to go hand-in-baby-bonnet with my questions about motherhood. Without a faith to grow in, the family unit is like a house built on sand. Though our faiths may differ in many ways, yours and mine, we are alike in the privilege and gift of faith we hold—a gem more to be treasured than life itself.

Being a Christian means, to me, that I'll never be alone again. The graces of my vocation and of my particular faith differ little from the graces of the vocation offered to mothers of every Christian faith. Mine surely has provided for me a few extras I've needed to fill out my own peculiar intellectual thick spots. Each Christian woman holds dear a faith tailored to her particular needs. But whatever our personal weaknesses and even the differences between your Christian faith and mine, we share them in Christ.

As women and mothers, we share in Christ, also, the weaknesses and problems of our husbands and of each child. Today Bill and I know that the responsibility for a child's training in life and in Christianity, as well as in discipline, belongs as much to the father as to the mother. The one who carries the most influence, I believe, is the one who spends the most hours and the most of him/herself on the child. Usually it is the mother.

This book is obviously intended for those who have opted for the usual routines of motherhood—for an option it is today. Yet now, before our last two children have left the nest, I find I have worked myself full circle until now I regard motherhood within the home, tempered in my case with stimulating church and community work, by far the best and most satisfying role *for me*. I'm presenting here our struggles, not because they're the only road to sanctity or even sanity. God knows all of us are always in a state of becoming, not of completion, while we're on this earth. This sharing with you is only because it distresses me to think of other parents suffering the same mistakes I made before some facts fell on me.

Other mothers have found other ways and yet others will seek further individual means to form for themselves the delicate Mary-Martha balance each of us must find if we are to reach our full potential in service to our families and completeness for ourselves in the doing.

2
Motherhood, Liberation, and Witness

No woman can ever be totally liberated, yet the one thing that can cause great unnecessary suffering for today's mother and her family is for her to continue to sit on the fence. For split decisions on personal-liberty issues can build divided homes, and with them divided loyalties and personalities. The truly content and tranquil woman, solid in her Christian faith and richly complete within herself, is the one who strives, however successfully or unsuccessfully, toward the Mary-Martha balance.

Whether we like it or not, women *are* freer today than they have ever been. But all freedom brings with it responsibilities equal to its joys. We who for so long had no choice now must not only choose but abide by our decisions afterward. *We must realize we cannot have it both ways.* We cannot reject without in turn facing rejection. We cannot run without leaving something behind. We cannot say our body is ours alone and still have someone with whom to share it.

We hear on every side that what we, as individual women, want and need must come first and of course it should, *to a point.* To the point of the basic needs of our husbands and children. To call desertion of our families liberation is unreal and, besides, it doesn't work. For we can't desert ourselves and if we have *ever* loved them, a part of us will always remain with them and return to haunt us.

To speak of keeping a house and making a home, even according to the relaxed standards of today, we still roll back time 2,000 years. *Do* our homes differ so completely from Mary and Martha's at Bethany?

In structure and conveniences, almost certainly. In service to families' basic needs, very little. Whether we use a broom and mop to clean and wood or branches to cook and heat, whether we use an electric floor cleaner, waxer, and polisher and an electric push-button stove and automatic furnace to heat, our floors still must be made to shine. Even frozen food must be warmed and eaten from clean dishes. Shelter is still only comfortable when heated.

A part of our lives, be we businesswomen or homemakers, is bound, irrevocably and daily, to the scut work that nobody likes. For if we do not do at least our half of the family's total work for basic needs, someone we love is being left to hold the unwashed dishes, the mop, and the diapers.

However sweet and lovable, babies are still very inconsiderate and often dirty creatures. Will I *ever* forget one day as we were living in Sitka, Alaska? All *I* had to do while Bill worked eight hours a day on a new naval base nearby was to keep up the tiny two-room house and care for our first baby, then eleven months old. Surely, some would say, I could have cleaned the entire twenty-by-twenty-foot house in two hours a day and had leisure to spare. But life doesn't give us what we'd like.

I had not the luxury of a washing machine, nor room to put it in, if I'd had one. So I sloshed the baby's clothes up and down in a washtub in the middle of the kitchen floor with a bathroom plunger for a "gyrator." Even so, I liked being in Alaska. It was an adventure and the plunger *did* do a fair job. But this one day the baby had been quiet too long. I went to the bedroom to see if all that silence was really sleep.

Mothers have acute senses of disaster and I was no exception, for the silence had suddenly become ominous.

The view that met my eyes made me want to turn and run crying, or beat my head against the wall, or whale the daylights out of the baby. But I only began to laugh, and then to dissolve in hysterical giggles. Being fairly new to motherhood, I'd carelessly pinned his diaper with only two pins, one on either side. Now I saw he had soiled the diaper and, being wide awake, had begun to play in it. For he'd smeared the feces on the sheet. And on the mattress. And the bars of the crib. And the bottoms of his feet and between his toes. And his hands and between his fingers. And his clothes. And on his face. And in his hair. Yet from the middle of all this unholy mess his eyes were so innocent!

It seems to me *any* mother facing such a complete calamity would be a fool if she didn't first want to bawl and then to run away from it. I've done my share of feeling that way with catastrophes. Unfortunately, I've also learned that when you turn your back on disaster, it patiently waits—and dries and becomes harder to do and more disagreeable—*until you get at it.* There is no way to clean a baby but to clean the baby.

As I later had other children, and even discovered other ways of pinning diapers, every single one of them has found a way to get into the identical predicament. Babies are basic as all human beings are basic and we have to face it. Their needs must be cared for unless we want to revert to animals.

Eventually and feeling very put upon, I once again cleaned our son and plunger-gyrated his bedding and clothes and added *them* to the crisscrossed lines that hung through the kitchen. They were strung inside for the very good reason that it was pouring rain outside as it does more often than not in Sitka. No longer was today an adventure, but *now* I could sit down and rest. Right?

Wrong. For when I tried it, the coal stove that had been

converted to oil and which often became red hot around its belly now belched, exploded, and coughed lids and door out into the room. The stovepipes crumpled into an inglorious heap, spewing dust and ashes and black spidery clouds all over. They covered not only the baby's laundry but the ceiling, walls, and everything else I had to touch before I could get dinner and it was only an hour before time to begin cooking.

To you these may sound like exaggerations. They are not. Unless my life is an exaggeration. Which it may very well be at that.

It's just that when I say *basic* needs, I mean there *do* exist needs so fundamental, so primary, that it takes help from on high to see us through them, or even to help us understand why they have to happen to *us*. Philosophy is fine, but "I *will* do it, but only for you, Jesus," often makes more sense.

Today even more is expected of us, for we have begun to analyze ourselves, and that brings everything we stand or fall for into painfully sharp focus. We are forcing ourselves into a facing up to, a reassessment of, our lives. In this reassessment of values we need to examine how we're fulfilling the spiritual needs of our children to whom we may have been so close we've lost sight of their needs. Have we, maybe, offered them gifts (money?) *instead of ourselves?*

We need to measure ourselves today *not* by our own terms, but by the terms Jesus made conscience-binding for men when they were the sole breadwinners: "Render therefore to Caesar the things that are Caeser's, and to God the things that are God's" (Matt.22:21). Too often these days we make money the hub of our lives, when the hub should be God himself.

For a few years there, dad brought home the bacon and when mom worked outside of her home, it was for short periods of time and only for the gravy. No more. Many women now spend full working days away from home, and unless you are among the wealthy few, this *always* means something at home left undone. No matter how liberated, we are only finite human beings with very real limits to our energy, our time, and our concerns. Far too often, as we become busier and busier (Marthas, whether in the house or at the office), the things we let slip while we try to do both are the attention and giving of ourselves which belongs to our children and our husbands.

Many have fled their homes for the marketplace to find themselves, only to learn after awhile that they have just changed one routine monotony for another. Unless you have to work outside the home, it doesn't seem a satisfactory choice. For marketplaces are noisier, more pressured, and more dull than any home. And no woman on a job has as much control over her own fate as she has as a homemaker.

There's a lot more love, and therefore more real living, in feeling the soft, warm arms of your small child wrapped around your neck "Just 'cause I wuv you, Mommy!" than all the bonuses and psychological strokes dispensed at the office in the name of good interpersonal relations.

We homemakers, Marthas by circumstance and vocation, busy ourselves about many "necessary" worldly things like diapers, oil smoke disasters, and how to stretch the money. Only—it is so terribly easy to work our way *away* from God in small nibbles, as did the sheep for which Christ searched with such tender care.

Tying love of God into worldly things sounds contradictory, sometimes almost sacrilegious. But our Creator made us the way we are, and tending to our basic needs will always remain a prerequisite, as will loving him as fully as we can as Mary-Marthas, if we are to return our torn world to God.

It's important to think our lives through, decide what and how we want to benefit others in our families as well as ourselves. Today's mother is caught and compressed between the real woman she is and the choices of several tantalizing other occupations dangled before her in the name of selfhood. Not all of the latter are valid by any means. This is a problem vital to every member of her family. No wonder she's tired. No wonder she thinks in circles. No wonder she's as emotional as the old "female image" made us all out to be!

Because whether you work at an outside job or whether you stay at home as a full-time homemaker—and whether you like it or not—authorities agree that *you, the mother of the family, are the image of God to your children*. Through any other source his love comes to them dimmer and with far less staying power. We mothers, *of our very selves*, are an inspiration to our children and our husbands. We are the warmth and brightness of Christ as our children will come to see him and place their values and their lives in his hands and his words.

The more love for our Lord we radiate, the more his truths can shine through us. And to radiate the warmth of his rich love, we must first be heated by it ourselves. If we are not actively growing, seeking to increase our love and service to him daily, if we are not lay apostles, we are slipping backwards. If we are not teachers of truth and love and Christ, then what kind of teachers are we?

For teach we do, in what we say and, more importantly, in what we do and are. None of us is worthy of being God's representative before humankind, let alone before those we love the most. Yet that's the job he's given to mothers. Neither are we worthy of guiding others' lives until they can guide their own. Yet for the years our children have been loaned to us, we must guide them or they'll fall behind or stray to the side.

On *our* faith rests the future faith of our children. If we are cold, we have no faith to offer. If we are lukewarm and feel that may be enough, see what our Lord had to say about being lukewarm: "So, because you are lukewarm, and neither cold nor hot, I will spew you out of my mouth!" (Revelation

3:16). And our children, like so many sponges, will absorb or be turned off by our lukewarmness in all its insipidness.

Ours is a humbling and terrible responsibility. When at first I failed to see the joys, but was only overwhelmed by the awesomeness of the tasks ahead of me in rearing children, I almost threw in my diaper pail.

I decided to read up instead. I devoured magazines and books to learn how to do this job right. I didn't realize in those days that what a mother *is* is far more important than what she *does*. My identical twin and I were the youngest of three children, so I'd had no experience with babies and the more I read, the more my sense of helplessness was reinforced. Today I know much of the material I read then was invalid, but in those indiscriminating days I figured any "authority" knew more than I.

According to the professionals quoted by our communications media, our society at that time expected me—not Bill—to be the catchall for every other family member's social, spiritual, and moral life, or their respective copouts. All this and I was also and somehow to keep my husband's ego high and my own appearance devastating enough to be an attractive sex partner and, no matter how many children, to have the house immaculate at all times. It was a period when cleanliness was not considered *next* to godliness, it was often idolized *as* godliness.

Yes, I've served my apprenticeship in scut work. I've cooked, nursed, chauffered, cleaned appliances and house, advised deaf teen-agers, wiped noses and bottoms, and done the general moral and physical homemaking jobs required by a family, but in those days they were required of *mothers* alone.

On one of my more depressed days after our last baby, I multiplied, added, and subtracted. It only made me more depressed to learn that in my life I have prepared over 10,070 bottles of baby formula, and have washed some 25,580 diapers without benefit of diaper service or disposables. And I even nursed two children for a time.

Yet I *never quite* met the magnificent standards of those days. But then the only woman I ever knew who had a large family and did meet them had a bleeding ulcer and was the rug on which the others wiped their feet.

In every woman's distaste for washing diapers, we often fail to appreciate the luxury we have. Our babies *have* diapers! And pins.

How well I remember the day I rinsed and then washed four dozen diapers whose condition had only deteriorated by having been left waiting so long. I wailed to myself in self-pity about why *I* should have three kids in diapers at once and why should *I* have to do this. Later the same day, as I pushed the baby downtown in his carriage with two toddlers holding the buggy at each side, I met a sober-faced friend whose baby was not yet three months old.

"How's the baby coming along, Frank?" I asked.

Tears filled his eyes and he dashed them away. "I'm just coming from the hospital," he said. "The baby's been there three days with a kidney infection." His eyes finally met mine. "I'd give my very *soul* for just *one* wet diaper! If her kidneys don't begin to work within twenty-four hours, the doctor says she'll die."

Later we heard she had died . . . and you may be sure that father's agony rose up to haunt me for a long time, each diaper-washing session. It's so *easy* to forget that blessings don't all come with identifying flags on them.

Would you believe many mothers, even in this day and age, and who have had the means to buy diapers, do not know about safety pins? When I had twelve children, I spent a strange and humbling day showing migrant workers' wives how to use a safety pin. They had been folding diapers in triangles, then tying them into a knot. The poor babies had had to sleep everywhere but on their stomachs.

No one can knock housekeeping, even today, and stay reasonably clean. We all live in houses and there's no possible way to escape at least half of the drudgery after we're married. But we have to find and live within our limits as persons, too.

Today we hear far too often how *un*important having a family is. That motherhood is for those who want it and thanks, but no thanks. Only—what about the family unit if we reject *a* family? Multiplied, *a* family becomes *a* society. Each time I hear the family as a unit put down, I think again of Watergate and of the discussions that have sprouted on every side about the moral breakdown of the country. They can cause us to react in either of two ways. We can stomp our feet and scream about the dishonesty of politicians. Or we can realize that all politicians, all leaders of our country, are men and women who were once very small children; and those who slid into dishonesty the first time they were offered power or money or both unless they scuttled their consciences may have had feeble ones to begin with. Consciences don't spring full-grown into our minds when we reach adulthood.

I keep wanting to ask, *"What kind of home did he/she come from?"* Membership in a formal religion is commendable and politically prudent, but *what kind of a home did he/she come from?* A good record of past business successes and community involvement is what often gets him/her elected. *But what kind of home did he/she come from?*

The more families strive to build honest young people strong in the love of God, the faster our society will return to one we can be proud of. The family is the first block, the cornerstone that holds society steady or lets it tip and tumble.

It is up to loving mothers to get that family unit back into its proper place of importance in today's world. *I know!* There *are* all the babies to bathe, and the cooking and dishes to do, and the house seems like a giant magnet set up just to attract dirt. How can we be partially Marys when our children need so much physical care? How can we be both a Martha with kids underfoot and patience shredded over that quarrel about a lost shoe—and a Mary, serene of heart, fulfilled and replenished daily be meditation on her place in God's universe?

We'd find it easier if we had not been falsely trained to see life through a male viewpoint. Education has set up masculine views inside of us and they're difficult to kick. The sharp rise in mental illness, in neuroses, in hypochondria and its resulting drug abuse, and in divorce may be traced in woman, at least in part, to the tragic attempt our society has made to cram her into a male mold.

Even those of us who have not quite accepted the male role have almost totally bought the publicity we read on Mother's Day cards. The *good* mother, we read, is that nebulous being who never needs sleep, never flies into a tizzy, or sees the most obvious flaws of her husband. A ghostly creature without personal feelings, without ego or time or inclination for her own growth.

After marriage and particularly after motherhood, when reality descends on the normal woman, the result *has* to be a gnawing guilt that creeps in. A burden of guilt which also confuses the entire role of motherhood until we feel defeated before we begin, even as we're programmed for change, one way or the other. Painful change.

With strange logic, our society has assumed that woman, with the biological advent of motherhood, automatically drops that competitive spirit her parents and teachers so enthusiastically encouraged in her teens. New confusions and disappointments move in. For motherhood not only eliminates all competition except for those too young to run the race. At the same time, it also makes a woman feel like a carnival barker with only two balloons and six children clamoring for them.

Result? That all-important *liking* for yourself as a person, which psychologists say is the most vital part of mental health, takes a nosedive. As we come smack up against new experiences for which our education and training have ill prepared us, we feel helpless. We try to go it alone and we stumble. Everyone does.

What we need to understand, but often fail to, is that the wisdom of Christ is with us all the way and can draw us through safely. Did he not say, "Let not your hearts be troubled; believe in God, believe also in me" (John 14:1)? When we once fully realize how near and real he is, the seemingly insurmountable perils of parenthood diminish like breakers dwindling on a peaceful beach until at last nothing remains but a trickle of the former fear—the reality of it gone.

None of us can succeed according to God's measure until we first try using his yardstick. If all mothers—and mother substitutes—could come to share with God their problems as well as their children, the beauty of the family and its attraction for others would beam outward like sound waves that never stop. Tremendous graces are waiting to be let in. Jesus is knocking. Why do so few answer the door?

Most of us are taught that God dwells within us in some way. Often we forget him when the little ones come along and we get more and more busy about many things. So busy we fail to see that being a Martha is not—was not even in Jesus' time—enough. We can't go it alone. Didn't our Lord remind Martha that Mary's loving awareness of him was the better portion?

As long as the youngsters need us, we will remain partly a Martha. Yet somewhere deep in the heart and consciousness of every woman stirs, too, a spark of divine wisdom teasing to be understood, calling her also to become a Mary. Mary—a woman who need not worry over material *or* spiritual problems.

If you haven't felt the spark, have you struck the match by finding time to be still and listen to your Creator? A retreat is one way. Another is to make time at home to be alone with him, either by reading Sacred Scripture or by just listening. Being busy about many things is a more common hazard today than when Martha used it as an excuse; and even today, *it results in not hearing what Jesus is saying.*

Anyone can budget time to listen if she wants to badly enough. Could you spare an hour if your pastor knocked at the door? Or your husband's boss? Or your mother-in-law? Or your parents? Then why not your Father in heaven?

Always within us are the ingredients for that well of peace that is the rich sense of belonging to God. The only way our souls, our problems, and our lives can be wrenched from our Lord is by the audacious act of our own turning away. We can *not* turn *him* away. We can only turn ourselves around until we no longer see him.

All of us suffer anxiety, agitation, and mounting tensions occasionally. Such symptoms for some become a life hazard. But often it signals insufficient attention to Jesus. Sit down at his feet, Martha, and *listen*—and learn how to relax and be at peace.

3
Real Love Is Discipline

Mothers seeking to follow Christian teachings are easily led into quagmires of permissiveness by other parents, teachers, and authorities who seem to know better than they what is right for their child. But it isn't so.

Our most difficult job these days is to take our *own* stand—ours and our husbands'—when it's against society's "values" of the moment. One of these highly prized but false values, we've learned, is the strange notion that permissive parents produce the happy child. Or that active discipline, as in paddling or removal of privileges, is bad for the child's personality. I fell heavily for the last ones.

Each set of Christian parents comes to parenthood equipped with God's graces and it may seem superfluous to have to say it, but graces are active forces, not just something we talk about in church.

One day I was at the home of a highly respected professional woman, a social worker and a counselor in the Los Angeles high schools for fifteen years. We were drinking coffee and chatting when her five-year-old son came in and asked, "Mom, can I go to the Johnson's to play?"

His mother looked doubtful.

"Just an hour?" he persisted.

Again she hesitated, then finally nodded, still skeptical. "But be sure and return by five. Tell Mrs. Johnson to send you home in an hour."

Something about her hesitancy made me ask, "Has being a social worker helped you be a better mother?"

She shook her head. "I wish it did. No, I often think of my own parents and what I valued most about their teaching my brother and me. They had a marvelous confidence in themselves and what they believed. *Parents must have confidence in themselves,* or their children will feel their doubts and immediately move in to take advantage. Yet I've personally seen too many problems in family living, through my profession. Right or wrong, my parents always *knew* they were right and that gave us children a very important sense of security; whereas I simply cannot be that sure."

"Right or wrong, they knew they were right. . . ." *Is* that always the best?

Of course not. But it does beat wavering. Just as "My country right or wrong" is far from the ideal attitude but surely beats its other extreme—running from the problems, the support and correction of one's country's ills. In both cases, it seems far more logical to look at the problem where it *and you* are at, and do the best you can.

This woman's attitude has helped me to do my best to be consistent. To try to eliminate the wavering in our family, even when we err and slip and later feel guilty.

But from errors we learned another magic trick. When a mother apologizes to her child for being wrong or unjust, the child learns that parents are human beings, too, and that mom loves the child enough to share her humanness with him/her. Sharing our faults with our loved ones is but another facet of love, especially the Mary love.

After watching my friend's motherhood at work, my short-lived envy of professional knowledge drained away. In no way am I a psychologist, except by the old tried and true method of experience.

As I see it, many of today's parents seem grouped into two camps, the permissive and the abusive. Both seem fanatic fringes of the same two-sided coin—rejection of the child, whether hidden or open. We've seen disasters from both treatments by people so close to us we've known their family situations.

What is *your* reaction, as a mother, when you ask your son, four, to do something and he stomps his foot and screams, "No! I won't!" Isn't four awfully young for a child to be defying you, the much bigger and, one hopes, wiser parent? Yet four-year-olds are doing it every day, while their mothers either pretend they don't hear or comment on how the child must be given his chance to express himself. Maybe so, but when mom stands by and condones, the day may come when she will realize this is only lax permissiveness— lack of respect for authority. Then when she belatedly attempts to enforce a rule vital to the child's health or welfare—real discipline at last—too late the child will have gone parent-deaf.

It's terribly easy for us to let the tail wag the dog. In fact much permissiveness may be simply taking the easy way out instead of actual rejection of the child.

I remember well the time one of our youngsters defied me and yelled, "No! I want my box *this* way!" as he jammed his toys into the chest "his" way. And I let him—because I was so tired! There'd been other times, too, when he refused to say his prayers, and I had had three hours' work to do in one, and I'd let him go. Another time when I was entertaining friends, it was so much easier to let the three-year-old stay up as she insisted, instead of making her take her regular nap.

Little things? No—because the slipshod phrase "kids will be kids" means, *to them*, seeing how far they can go and just exactly where those limits *are* that real love sets up.

I feel particularly sorry for the poor child whose problems begin to multiply when he begins to catch on to the sad truth that persistent lack of discipline most often is misguided, or a lack of any real love. And make no mistake—youngsters catch on to that very thing! You can't fool a growing child about your deepest emotions any more than you can a baby.

One example of sorry lack of discipline showed the day we went to a church potluck where part of the entertainment was a movie for children. I sat on the fringe of the group holding our smallest child. The last table was behind me. Suddenly I felt someone tapping against the back of my chair. I was tired and the tapping annoyed me. I turned around, and there was a boy about five, sitting on *top* of the table. His mother, a well-dressed woman with a determinedly patient face, stood directly behind him. She noted my look, patted his head, and said automatically, "Don't kick the chair, Johnny."

Johnny stopped for a second and then renewed the kicking with a little more force. There was no sound from the mother until I squirmed again. Then she said a little louder, "Johnny, won't you *please* get down from the table and stop kicking the nice lady?"

By this time I was *not* feeling like a nice lady, but I'm a little stubborn and, besides, I wanted to see if Johnny would ever get his comeuppance. The movie lasted a full hour and so did the kicking, while Johnny's mother was oblivious to her obligation to make her son see the light—even if that meant placing the emphasis on the seat of his pants.

Another time I was having a cup of coffee late one summer morning at a friend's home and her little boy, seven, was playing around our feet. The boy began to hit me hard on the calf of one of my legs. I moved the leg, but he only slithered over closer and hit me again while his mother, whose feet were down there somewhere, too, appeared to be completely unaware of the boy.

As I looked under the table to see what was going on, I tried to be obvious, but she paid no attention. Since she did not, he hit me harder, apparently for attention. There was no defense left me, except what has always been woman's best defense, her mouth. "Ouch!" I exclaimed. "That hurt!" And I rubbed my leg.

Finally, and only because I'd made such a scene, his mother sighed and said, "Philip! You get out from under the table! What are you doing down there, anyway?" And that was the end of it. No further comment or apology came, from either mother or child.

I said no more about it and neither did she, but little Philip walked away from the scene with a very satisfied smirk on his face. *He* was running that family and he knew it, yet he was one of the unhappiest little boys I've ever known. He grew into as pesky and unlikable a teen. The last I heard of him, he had been arrested for grand theft and was at a diagnostic center awaiting placement.

Every mother needs to remind herself—and often—not to permit her offspring to drive, goad, or push her around, no matter what the age or sounds—as in the case of that most put-upon soul, the teen-ager, who usually has a well-developed talent for conning mom by the time he/she's fourteen.

I asked our fifteen-year-old daughter one day to clean the basement. She nodded but sat immobile as a Buddha until I forgot about it. The next day I asked her again, but this time she was glued to the television and I tired of waiting for the station break. Besides, I was still trying to keep the peace, so I didn't insist.

The third day I'd had it. "Get at that basement, young lady," I exploded, "and *now!*"

She stuck out her lower lip and asked innocently, "Did you tell me before?"

Right then, I realized this was not the mature-looking woman she often looks, but the infant into whose skin she crawls periodically. "Yes," I sighed, "I've asked you three

times now. And I won't take excuses or back talk. Just get on
the ball and clean that basement."

She sulked all the way downstairs. Ten minutes later she
was singing. An hour later, she came up the stairs
besmudged and perspiring and wiping loose hair back from
her grinning face.

"You know what, Mom?" she asked. "It feels kind of good
to have you make me get to work. You know, I sort of have
this hangup, this tendency to put off doing things and you
should *just see* that basement now!"

But my experiences and lapses in discipline go back to our
first child. As I've said, I was one of three children and had
had no contact with babies before my own came along.
Naturally, then, my first unsettled years of parenthood
blossomed into all sorts of problems brought on, I learned
much later, by my own permissiveness. For at first I slavishly
followed the books on child guidance which advised reasoning with one's child instead of corporal punishment. According to those books, "Just because I said so!" was a deadly
sin. It took a long time to learn that *it's sensible to reason just
so long.* Any more, and the kid is using it to back *you* into a
corner.

As our first child grew older, if he hit another little boy
with a pail and shovel, I was afraid to paddle him and afraid
to scold. I used persuasion only. I was *very* careful not to
break his spirit, though Bill, one of twelve children, assured
me again and again that spirits don't break all that easily.
Finally I tried coaxing—and our son, intoxicated by his
power over me, hit *me* with the pail!

But God is good. He gave me another baby and another
chance to learn—and another—and another, until out of
necessity and self-defense, I began erecting moral fences to
keep the kids from killing each other as well as me.

There are other mothers who learn the hard way as I did,
and the worst thing about that is that the older children are

the poor guinea pigs while the parents learn what it's all about. A friend of ours who has eight children claims babies should be like fish so you could throw them back until you'd learned how to care for them right.

Isn't it too bad that parents never learn all there is to know about child training? I know we still seek help when and how we can find it, and there are only two still at home.

The most gratifying thing about discipline is that the young person who receives it feels safer and more loved than he did without it. Child abuse is the opposite in every way. Child discipline is *never* child abuse. One causes a happy, loved child. The other produces fear and a battered child and shouts loudly to family and neighbors alike that this mother (or father) has no control over herself *or* her child.

Parents who find it impossible to control their intense anger at the child owe it to that youngster, and to themselves, to seek professional help. For we—and our children—learn self-control when we're very young *by the example of self-control we see in our parents.* I'm convinced parents who abuse their children are as distressed as the children, but simply don't know which way to turn. They're afraid.

If you *or* your spouse is caught in this web of uncontrollable temper, fear of discovery should be the least of your worries. Fear for the kind of life you're laying out for your child's future should drive you to seek help *and fast.*

But ordinary discipline—the center of these two extremes—builds strength and character in a child. There are positive ways of saying no as well as negative, but our children only learn it by seeing it happen. A positive *no* is one intended to produce positive results, a negative *no* is said either for no good reason or just to make sure the youngster knows you're bigger and in control. If this is what it takes for them to realize you're in control, you're not, you know.

Some years back a boy made the headlines with his vandalism and delinquency, and was quizzed by a reporter who asked why he'd destroyed so much property. The boy said he'd never had a licking in his life. And to him that meant his folks didn't care one whit about him. If the police turned him loose now, he threatened he would just do it all over again and keep it up until one or the other of his folks cared enough about him to spank him!

Out of the mouths of babes. And *this* babe was ten.

I'll never forget how astonished I was the night I spanked our six-year-old boy who had always been reasoned with, whether reasoning worked or not. He stormed away from me, shocked and angry. But *within minutes*, the tears still standing on his freckled cheeks, he sidled back through the door and over to me, threw his arms around me as if he were drowning, and gulped, "I love you, Mommy. I'm sorry."

He was secure. I could see it in every freckle.

Making your point with a child must be much like finding a lost shoe in a family of fifteen. Losing tempers never helps. Throwing things never helps. Screaming like a fiend never helps. I know. I've tried all three. Both the lost shoe and the lost point show themselves when you cease to fight them *and* when you least expect them.

I hardly remember what it's like to have two or three children. Sometimes it seems we've had our thirteen forever. But I've learned now that when the small fry threaten to drive me out of my mind (and ten or six or even two can do it), it's only because I've allowed myself to cease, for the moment, to function as a mother. We have slipped again into a pseudo-family composed only of children, large and small, and all trying to have their own way.

A real family is a unit with children and a pair of guiding parents to point up straight thinking and obedience. Before a child can learn to obey the Ten Commandments, he has to learn to obey.

To be, today, both the Martha who tends to the physical needs and the Mary who is our children's pattern for godliness is extremely hazardous and many times thankless and we couldn't survive it without a loving Lord. But with his help, we are forming Christians. Isn't that worth it? It may take twenty years to complete the job, but some day twenty years will seem short.

Each of us mothers is unique and precious to God. Our souls, *our true beings,* are a very part of the living Christ we represent to society and to our families. We've picked the hardest vocation in the world—but the most rewarding even day by day, when we hang in there and offer to our children the only answers in this world for them *or* us: Obey our Lord's commands, the most important of which is that we love others as we do ourselves.

We *can* rear responsible young Christians in today's insane world—when love is expressed in necessary discipline as well as in approval when it's earned. It helps one avoid guilt, to realize as you apply discipline to a child, that you are defying all of the outside influences that reach him. Be honest about it. We're attempting to teach him/her exactly the opposite of what this world believes. No wonder it's difficult. But it's easiest when we begin by seeing that the world's "values" have brought it to its present chaos and that only God and our finding ourselves through him can make it better.

Besides, when we surround our duties with an aura of love for our Lord, the load miraculously lightens. The door to that aura (the Mary locked within each of us) will easily swing open when you find and use the balance that allows time for yourself and God alone. Time planned for each day, whether it be to read Sacred Scripture, to meditate, or to rest, *but rest with God.*

More—after that first door opens, another will swing away too. Your own quiet personal relationship with God will bubble up until it spills over into other areas of your life—and the working load will have become a working prayer.

As Marthas, we may long to leave the world and retire as Mary did, to a place of silence and seclusion. Only I don't know any silent families unless the kids are sick. But we *can*, and for our sakes and theirs we should, find our prayer where we find our work. To love as we live. To become Mary-Martha mothers in a God-like sense.

4

You Can't Fool a Baby

The difficulty with trying to strike a Mary-Martha balance in one's life is that we tend to keep teetering on the tightrope. The first thing we encounter while trying to develop into a good Christian mother, a Mary-Martha, is the baby, right? For with that new child of God comes both love and problems. Many of our habits in caring for children we form according to our own upbringing and the doctors' instructions until it seems an automatic know-how that helps us over the first nervous weeks of learning about this wee bit of humanity.

Then we hit a snag. No child comes with a parts kit telling us how to put his life foundation together, yet that is our, the mothers', job. So we struggle for a pain-filled period, wallowing in a sea of helplessness, fearing we've lost everything we've ever learned about kids.

Suddenly our struggle to develop self takes a back seat and we don't even realize that in this turning outward we *are* developing. For human beings only *really* find themselves through other human beings. That's why a Christian mother's fullness as a follower of Christ is built step-by-pain-and-error-step, as she is forced by circumstance (and God?) to turn outward from herself to the child.

When I came to the realization that I didn't love one of our middle children, any concerns I had over *me* vanished, except for a terrible guilt that I had brought this disaster upon little Billy (*not* his real name, because while the children know the story, I've never told them which one it was). For during the months I carried him and as he was delivered, there was no single circumstance or group of them that could have been a contributing factor. All had been quite normal. I came to feel I no longer knew anything about children, and with this conviction, my own sense of value and self-respect crumbled. When that happens, you feel there is no more balance and this, too, comes through clearly to the children.

Early on, however, mothers learn that when it comes to their own emotions, a baby or a child can spot a phony every time. The nervous mother produces a nervous baby. The insecure mother produces a whiny, insecure, and sometimes colicky baby. No matter how calmly you *act* at such a time, your real emotions come through to him loud and clear.

It took what I thought was a very unusual experience to force me to face my own emotions as nothing at that time yet had. I was burping Billy when I read in a book on child care of the vital connection between a baby's emotions and his mother's. Until that moment I had not realized its importance. After all, what mother would need to mask her emotions? I'd loved all of the others with that spontaneous affection every parent is expected to feel.

But this day I pulled Billy away from my shoulder and looked unhappily into his wide face. A ready smile beamed back at me, his blue eyes clear and guileless. He was a lovable baby. He deserved more than I'd given him. Because for some unexplainable reason, *I could not feel any love for this baby.* I had tried. But I knew I was failing him, because you can't fool a baby. Not really.

I shifted him to the other shoulder and closed the book

with a frustrated sigh. "Dear God! What can I do?" I whispered, and needed an answer more than I ever had in my life.

The chapter I'd been reading on emotional illness in children had shaken me badly. Emotional stability was becoming ever more important as increasing strains of perfectionist living bore down on our family as it did on others. Mental illness, the author said, stemmed from a lack of love on the part of the parents. Another unkind generality that has caused untold damage even to innocent parents, I've since learned.

But that day I believed it and a flash of guilt seared my conscience. Was Bill's love great enough to overcome the fact that I felt absolutely *no* affection for our baby? I knew it could not be. Like most fathers, he was gone too much of the time.

Our baby was already two months old and the dislike, or more accurately, the *nonfeeling* I'd felt for him from the moment the nurse first laid him into my arms at the hospital had only increased by the day while I cared for him meticulously. I patted his back. Could some natural obstacle have caused me to be this way? I asked myself repeatedly. No.

Then what was wrong with me?

I'd tried so very *hard* to feel affection for him. Billy was not neglected, left to cry his heart out, or even left alone. It was simply that I could not love him, felt no emotion toward him at all.

He burped loudly, and then with conscientious but cool care I changed him, placed him back in his crib, and returned to the book which had brought the problem into such vivid focus.

"Babies need love. It's such a simple answer."

But it was not simple! Please, Father in heaven, show me how to love him! Everyone knew love was the open door into a child's mind and heart. But with this baby I hadn't been able to open that door. And on this, I dared not confide in anyone else. I was too ashamed.

From the first time I'd held him in the hospital, I'd forced myself to give him awkward, artificial caresses which had come to nothing. I think I'd known all along they were futile. The only real love our baby knew was the quiet murmuring he heard from his father in the evening or during the night when he awakened, for Bill has always helped me with he children at night. We called it our "shared time." But since Billy had come along, I found myself turning away from Bill as I held the baby, so he wouldn't notice how impersonal I felt. It was as if I wore a huge sign. I was so sure he'd see my unnatural coldness.

And now this—this chapter on emotional illness in children. No mother could care more than I for her children to grow strong, emotionally as well as physically. Yet I sat there, distressed and with not the faintest idea what to do.

I remembered a parents' meeting I'd attended a year before. On the panel had been a psychiatrist who specialized in children's problems. One of the parents asked him, "How can you know whether you're getting through to your child? I try to teach my son something and months go by and it seems as if I'm getting nowhere."

The doctor had only grinned engagingly. "That's no sign he hasn't heard you. I'd say don't give up until you've tried for at least seven years. It sometimes takes that long to get through, even with a normal, intelligent child."

I'd been shocked. Seven years was such a long time. But now, facing a much more important problem, the seven years seemed like a reprieve. At least, I thought, I have time. I'll do everything I possibly can.

So I began. Since before our first baby, I'd been an avid reader of authorities on child care, but now my education in motherhood took on new depth. I began an intensive search for every minute way in which I might go "the extra mile." *Surely, God, there's some way to help Billy!*

Meanwhile, I decided it couldn't hurt to take advantage of each tiny speck of emotion I did feel. *Maybe, please God, I can build on what little there is?*

As if in answer to my prayers I found, now that I was alerted to them, that there *were* fleeting moments when Billy's broad smile or a touch of his chubby hand evoked a response. They had been so slight before that I had not even recognized them. A sliver of hope moved through me and was gone. It was too little to build on. *Wasn't it?*

But there was nothing else to do. So painstakingly I taught myself to respect each passing feeling and respond quickly, before the emotion shifted again to the familiar one of dislike. This process took self-control, but it required even more to thrust away the awful, growing guilt that all but smothered me. I felt as if I'd turned into a monster and dared not reveal it.

Sometimes I held the guilt at bay. Often I didn't succeed. But I *was* feeling some responses to Billy, followed by my quick pats, squeezes, and a kiss, *but only when truly felt.* Because I was more acutely aware than ever that Billy would not be fooled by anything less than real affection.

Weeks dragged by and the short senses of satisfaction so rarely glimpsed were almost completely hidden by the certainty that they came too seldom. It was obvious Billy was sweet and everyone *else* loved him. Then why didn't I?

One day I was so completely overwhelmed by doubts and fears that I had to share my awful secret. I was hanging clothes on the line close to our neighbor. The next thing I knew we were chatting at the fence and I blurted it all out to her. To my surprise, she seemed intensely interested. Then, her face flushed, she confessed, "It's been the same way with me! I'd never have had nerve enough to mention it, if you hadn't first. *I was so sure I was a freak!* Bob and I even decided we wouldn't have any more children if I was such a poor mother. Do you *really* think it's different with different kids? With the same mother, I mean?"

"I *know* it is!" That much I knew because of our others, and it seemed to comfort her. While I, too, was immensely relieved by *her* confession. And I was to learn through the years that followed that many more women than anyone suspects suffer the same disaster, each one fearing, as I had, that she is alone and unique.

The first real progress in my new efforts came when I noticed a pattern beginning to form. At certain times of the day, especially the quiet ones when we were alone, I began to feel closer to Billy. They were still only seconds, but they were real and warm.

At first, bath times had been awful hours when his splashing and paddling until water covered the bathroom invariably made hot anger rise in me. With tightened lips and trying to hold my feelings in, I mopped the floor and worried. *What could possibly be wrong with me?* Then, only because it had to be done, I wrapped him in a wide, thick towel and rubbed his back, holding him close, heartbreakingly close, and felt—absolutely nothing. I tried very hard to replace my unfair anger with something else. Even detachment would be an improvement. *Dear God, he deserves more!*

Then, so slowly I didn't realize it at first, I began to watch the wriggling, cuddly water baby and occasionally I'd feel the urge to kiss his wet neck—and did, quickly, before the precious feeling dissipated again. It took a full month of such trying, interspersed with fervent prayers for help, before I felt my lips curve into a smile as I held Billy and knew another flash of actual *liking* for him. Gradually, now, the finish at bath time became times for a quick hug in return for the precious feel of the squirming warm dampness of him.

For all those long weeks I'd managed to keep my awful

fears and dreads, even my hopes, from Bill. I was so ashamed! Part of my attitude, my shame, I think had been formed when, as a child, I'd heard that people *fall* in love, any kind of love, as into a deep crevasse. It seemed that one had no control over this elusive emotion. So far as I knew, love was something that came to parents unsolicited and in full force, not small and to be built up over the years until it gained full stature. Hadn't Bill and I fallen in love at first sight?

Even as I began to sense progress when Billy and I were alone, my feelings for him were still so fragile anyone else's presence instantly caused them to vanish. There were terribly discouraging days—once even two weeks—when I felt no liking at all. Maybe I was trying to do the impossible. But knowing a tiny baby's emotional strength depended on the love he knew from Bill and me, I kept doggedly on, watching, praying. It was a very long time. Three months that felt like three years.

At last after trying for what seemed forever to build love out of nothing, I sat holding him once again in my arms trying to burp him. Suddenly both of his round grasping fists wound around my neck and hugged me tightly. And for the first time since he was born, a rush of love poured through me. I hugged him close, both believing and unbelieving, while one of his hands moved up to touch my wet cheek.

I loved him! I actually loved little Billy! For a moment, but just a moment, I loved him as fully as I did the other youngsters. A little of the relief that surged through me was all I dared feel. It still might fail—oh, surely not! My method *had* brought changes, hadn't it?

I renewed my efforts. With longer, caressingly longer time, I dressed Billy with great care and brushed his blond baby fuzz into a kewpie top. These, too, brought their reward. Before two days had passed another surge of real love came and went. Discouragement now completely disappeared. Eagerly I continued my pursuit of the elusive, intangible, but nonetheless real, love that had to be somewhere between us.

One never knows, actually, how much deep response is felt by a small baby. But having had the others, I was only very sure he'd know if I were faking.

By now I, a bustling and worried Martha, had developed a Mary's keen interest also in the emotional needs of children, my own and others. To learn more about this fascinating subject, I read and talked with teachers, doctors, and every authority who would hold still for questioning. Eventually my Martha-like anxiety brought me to an interview with a psychiatric social worker at the local child guidance center in our city. A slight man with bristly gray hair, a slow smile, and exceptionally shrewd eyes, who showed me into an office equipped with games and toys.

I asked him what was the effect on a tiny baby when he came to realize his mother or father didn't love him. He looked thoughtful, but his answer coincided with what I'd already learned with such difficulty. "It has a profound effect on his emotions. The tiny baby begins to react very early in life. The child's self-image is by and large developed upon those he loves—his parents. He finds himself by the way he is mirrored in them. If this feeling of love is impoverished when it comes to him, then so is his sense of self."

Overcome with awe at this statement of a mother's tremendous importance to her child, it was a moment before I asked, "Could—is a child *ever* untouched by knowing one of his parents does not love him?"

"No!" He was emphatic. *"Such a child could never be untouched.* There are many ways of showing and feeling love. Some parents set firm limits, show affection, are consistent. There are any number of ways, sometimes a composite of many. But these differ drastically from the misguided, too protective or overprotective or too permissive concept often mistaken for real love. In reality, the overprotective 'love' merely postures as love while taking the place of a deep feeling of threat the child represents to the parent."

I nodded thoughtfully. "So there are different reasons for a parent's rejection of a child, whether conscious or not?"

"Yes, but mostly parents *are* aware of their true feelings. The only exception might be if a child represented someone or something repugnant enough for the parent to keep his own feelings hidden from himself. He does this by rationalizing."

I needed to know one thing more. "Can parents be aided in facing these facts while the child is still young enough to be molded?"

"Certainly. That's the very core of our child guidance program." His arm gestured around the game-filled room. "And it's equally destructive to the child if his thinking becomes distorted and he *thinks* he's been rejected, whether or not it's true. Our kind of clinic could offer real help."

He went on to explain how parents often can help benefit children themselves, as I had done, if they are aware of the problem and capable of meeting it with success. He suggested, however, that the parent who has made such an attempt and still finds herself continuing the previous patterns should seek professional help. I left his office heartened that my efforts toward my own son had met with success and were being overcome without outside help.

Billy was almost six months old before I began to relax and enjoy him, happy in the feeling that I had accomplished much. But it was two years before a friend, glancing at snapshots of the children, exclaimed, "My, your children are lucky! You can just *see* the love shining in your face there, where you're holding Billy!"

I turned away from her, fearful of showing the naked gush of gratitude to Almighty God that had brought such "luck" to us. It had been a long time since I'd felt cold toward

Billy—but it was her remark which told me that I'd won an important battle with myself.

Today Billy has passed the turbulent teens and is a handsome adult in his twenties and yet sometimes he brings his problems to me. My concerns as he grew into adolescence came spontaneously, for my love had imbedded deeply and strongly enough to carry us both through those and the trying years every young man encounters as he steps into the world of his future.

When we're busy about our own many duties, it seems to me, it's terribly easy for us mothers to fool ourselves. It's only as we take a faltering step away from self that we stop and think about our baby—and our own inner being—and God. Even then we scarcely realize we're leaning on God as we never had before. A little bit of the Mary to balance the busy, busy duties.

We only increase our tensions by expecting a life of housekeeping and child caring to be easy. Unless we want to be full-fledged undiluted Marthas. And full-fledged undiluted Marthas are drudges. But then, nobody ever said being a Christian was *only* sniffing the daisies.

So what if much of Christianity goes against our "natural" grains? At least it helps us to avoid the dangers of becoming so totally aware of ourselves that our children's and our husbands' needs cease to exist in our world—the short, easy path to loneliness and serious gaps in any future human relationships. Families need mothers who reach outside of themselves, not those who close the door and keep themselves safe from the others.

To be a Christian is to be a very active apostle. For from family, we take another step outward. Some mothers we know cook one less meat meal a week for their families to conserve beef and, with it, grain for countries who don't have enough. Only a mother can implant in her child's heart the gift of giving and such an early start will bear fruit in world concern for a future that badly needs it.

There is an eternity of differences between unleavened motherhood—the mundane world of the Martha—and the deeply spiritual world of the contemplative Christian woman, the Mary. Striking the *perfect* balance is a neat goal—and great to strive for—but merely staying upright is important, too, and more reachable. For as I see it, the tightrope of Christian motherhood is balanced on the taut wire of fulfillment across a weary world where many women are chasing after rainbows without fully understanding that rainbows come only through gray skies and rain.

Balance is the key. That balance upon which depends the varying scales of our apostolic lives as Christian wives and mothers—and rich tranquil fulfillment for ourselves as children of God.

5

Your Child's
Looking-Glass Self

As Christian mothers, we automatically desire to build love for God in our children, because we know such love is far more important than worldly things. Seldom do we understand, as we set about the training of our little ones, that we are learning as much as they. Through trial and tumbling and failure, we are growing steadily in a balance between the Martha who has to be and the Mary who fills us with God's love and tranquillity.

As the balance develops, we become more keenly attuned to the sensitivities, the individual differences, between our children. And even while maintaining the discipline which alone develops loving responsible adults, we step carefully. For to our children, the parents, and especially we mothers, represent Almighty God. It's as if we are leaving on our children's psyches the thumbprint by which they will find or lose their God as they grow up.

The only way our children will be able to learn freely and easily to love and serve God is by our helping them to begin their lives by *liking themselves*. Such miracles do not come about of their own accord. A child's accomplishment is very much in the hands of the mother who is with him/her daily. Even the "working mother," who sees her children for shorter periods of time, can bring about the attitudes she wants her children to have by what she says and does and is. For she, as a person and as a mother, speaks more loudly than anyone else except their father, and unless both mother and father are working, he is often gone so much more that his impressions are badly weakened. Children care so deeply what we believe they're worth that their personalities are literally in our hands.

The psychiatric social worker told me that what our children see in their mirrors are the little people we parents see in them. If their goodness is reinforced by our loving support and by acceptance from brothers and sisters and other important loved ones, they gladly conform to this picture. If, on the other hand, either parent sees only bad in the child, he will learn to fit that mold. Our youngsters' reflection of themselves resembles our picture of them so accurately it's frightening. And humbling.

During a juvenile court hearing for their son, fourteen, one father we know stated flatly, "He may be my son, but he's a rotten kid just the same!"

The boy was there for petty theft. He'd been caught shoplifting and the store manager had insisted on pressing charges. The boy's mother, a quiet, mousy little woman who was afraid of her blustery husband, was beside herself. "I tried to tell Hugh he shouldn't say things like that about his own flesh and blood," she wailed to me. But she couldn't bring herself to stand up to her husband to help the boy.

Nor did the father change his attitude. The rantings and railings in their home went on. They lived a few blocks from us and the mother came to our house to blow off steam she might better have used to help her boy. For the father openly insisted he couldn't wait to get rid of the boy.

Well—he finally has. The years have shown how the man's certainty that his boy was rotten led to his disaster.

The son acted out that original image of the "rotten kid." He graduated from swiping paperbacks to "joyriding" in a stolen car, and finally to burglary. Today he's serving time in the state prison for grand larceny and his father is *still* telling anyone who will listen that it was all the boy's fault. That he "was born with a bad streak in him."

The little ones God loans us for eighteen precious years are born with very special personalities meant to grow to serve God in a unique way. But one rash, outspoken word can damage their image of themselves as surely as a brutal fist can crush out a bud before it has a chance to bloom.

Neither Bill nor I shall ever forget the awful time that followed an incident that happened when one of our daughters was three. Someone had carelessly told her, "You're a naughty girl!" instead of the less traumatic "That was a naughty thing to do!"

A very easy thing to let slip. Right? But far from simple in its repercussions. For it makes a tremendous difference toward a child's future development and self-image whether he commits a naughty *act* or is considered—by the parents who represent God to him—a naughty person.

I first realized something was wrong a few hours after I'd put our six children to bed and went later to check on them. Bonnie was still awake, huddled miserably in her bed, sobbing softly to herself. I pulled her into my arms and cradled her. "What's the matter, sweetheart? Tell Mommy."

Her glistening blue eyes looked up as tears slipped down the woebegone face and she gulped, "I want to be a gooood girl! I want to be a gooood girl!"

"But you *are* a good girl!" I hugged her close, trying to make this tiny child realize what a fine person she was. She, of all our kids, had always tried so hard to do the right thing. She sobbed and sobbed and only several hours later cried herself to sleep in my arms. When she awoke the next morning her bed was soaked—and she hadn't wet the bed for over a year.

"It's OK, Bonnie," I said quickly. "Everyone has accidents sometimes." I changed the bed without further comment, but her shame-faced blue eyes followed me around. Later she toddled behind me into the kitchen as I worked. It was upsetting to realize how *easily* she seemed to have accepted the tag someone had carelessly pinned on her.

The bedwetting continued and night after night she still sobbed herself to sleep, wailing over and over, "I want to be a gooood girl! I want to be a gooood girl!" Though I reassured her in every way I knew, nothing, not loving nor words, could change her mind.

She began to stutter and by this time I was in a frenzy. *Who had done this to her?* How had it all started? I quizzed the family, but all denied having even scolded Bonnie.

I visited the nursery school she'd begun to attend only weeks before the problem developed. But her teacher only shook her head. "Bonnie's a fine little tot. She hasn't given me a second's trouble."

I was at a dead end. Since neither Bill nor I is a psychologist, we couldn't decide exactly what to do. Nursery school was the only recent change in Bonnie's life. Maybe the safe, familiar background of home and love would help.

But nothing changed right away. It was several weeks before Janice, then five, sidled up to me one evening while I chopped cabbage for cole slaw and asked casually, as if she'd never heard the subject before, "Mommy, Bonnie's not a naughty girl, is she?"

I looked quickly at her. "Of course not. She's a sweet little doll." The strangeness on her face caused me to ask then, "Why?"

" 'Cause that's what the girl called her one day in nus'ry school."

"What girl, Janice?"

"The girl that goes to high school and that comes in in the afternoon to help the teacher." She munched on a cabbage leaf.

I tried not to let my concern show. "Why ever would she say a thing like that?"

"I don't know, Mommy. 'Less it was 'cause she wet her pants and the girl had to clean up the puddle."

We didn't go flail our fists at the nursery school. The damage was done. All we could do now was to alert every member of the family, again, that Bonnie needed a lot of very special loving until she, too, realized she was as fine a person as God had made in the first place.

The library was my next stop. There I read all I could find on personality disturbances. In psychology, I learned, they call it negative labeling. In church they call it rash judgment. In parenthood it's often thoughtlessness.

Call it what you will, it is fearfully damaging, *for labels never point just to the past.* They also point to the future. All of us, even adults, tend to conform to others' expectations of us. Remember the old childhood trick of telling someone he looked sick? In no time at all, he turned pale and often felt ill.

As with a mother's control over her children's beginning day, when our youngsters were very small, I had to watch myself. Mothers are barometers, too, of long-lasting family happiness.

Negative labels are deceptively easy to tack onto someone in a careless moment—and so terribly difficult to get rid of. In spite of all the love we lavished on little Bonnie, it was six full months before her stuttering stopped, and almost as long before she quit wetting the bed and sobbing herself to sleep at night, gulping out the most pitiful wail in the world, "I want to be a gooood girl! I want to be a gooood girl!"

Authorities say a mother's sensitivity to her child's feelings is crucial to his/her emotional health. But heartbreak can move in fast if we are not careful. Like love, heartbreak's repercussions roll outward to touch us all. Look what happens to the job of an excellent responsible worker when his employer learns he is an ex-convict. Or an ex-drug addict.

Or an ex-*any* label that boxes the person in so tightly that fellow human beings forget there ever was a God-Man who died to show us what forgiveness and love are all about.

Being a mother is the most love-demanding job there is. Even when we don't want or feel like giving of ourselves, there are the kids, wide-eyed and wide-eared, their emotions quivering with the need to know what we think of them. Soaking up every word, deed, and attitude they receive from us, who are their patterns.

Probably the most difficult thing I've had to learn as a mother is that it doesn't really matter *what* Bill or I actually say to a child or even what we mean. The only thing that counts is what we *communicate* to him when he hears it. Being an individual, he brings to our words preconceived ideas. Often his reaction comes from a misunderstanding of our words. It may come from a single word, as it did with one little four-year-old boy, the day his father began to clean his rifle.

The son stood nearby, looking on. Finally he said, "What are you going to shoot?"

"I'm going to kill a deer," his father replied.

"Oh." The word was very tiny, almost inaudible, and his father paid no more attention to him.

The man had been gone on his hunting trip for several hours before the little boy, one of four children, snuggled up close to his mother, his lower lip trembling.

"What's wrong, Bobby?" she asked.

He looked at her with dark eyes that swallowed up his face. "Mommy, which little dear is Daddy going to shoot?"

Children can hear us very clearly—yet pick up meanings and shadings of meanings until they hear something entirely different from our words. It's our responsibility as parents to keep our antennae up and maintain a keenly receptive ear and eye on our kids. Loving sensitivity to their feelings can show up the many little kinks they can get in their thinking as they try to sort familiar childlike reactions and under-standings from the strange, adult details to which they are constantly exposed.

There are many areas of child rearing that are nettles to handle. Being adopted is one, yet see how beautiful and in-sightful was one mother's way of handling it: Her daughter, three, had just learned she was adopted, and had failed to react one way or the other. This, the mother knew, could mean trouble. She didn't know what to do. Then one day the little girl watched her dress to attend a wedding.

"Mommy," she asked, "what's a wedding?"

Her mother was quick to reply, "It's when two people adopt each other and promise to love each other forever and ever no matter what they do."

She knew her little girl's looking-glass self was intact, adoption and all, the next day when she overheard her whisper into the cocker spaniel's silky ear, "I just wanted you to know I'm 'dopting you. That means I'll love you forever and ever, no matter what you do."

When the little ones are thus set firmly in respect and lik-ing for themselves, their mothers are well on their way to be-ing able to really guide them. And from mere teaching to teaching love of God becomes only another small step. A step which the Martha may be too busy to see is bringing her, too, closer to the peace of the loving Lord—the fulcrum upon which our own balance is steadied and supported. It is in a mother's formation of her children that her own life finds its balance. Together, the Martha and the Mary within her will some day form the beautiful combination that will enable her to be "in this world, but not of it."

6

Keep the Light Note

One of the most important factors in helping a child develop a healthy self-image is to teach him the fine art of laughing at him/herself. Whether or not children learn to laugh at themselves, depends entirely on whether mom is a chore-laden, unhappy drudge who is sure the world is doomed or whether she's found a little of the Mary balance and discovered that to be between a rock and a hard spot only means it's easier on the feet. That no kick is without a boost, even when it hurts. Mothers come usually in one category or the other. We can spend most of our time either laughing or crying.

Why puddle up when it only turns the day into a drizzle? A mother's happy disposition is like the rainbow over the clouds. The sunshine and bright colors are there to see, and beautiful. Why keep our noses so far down we see only the heavy gray of the lower clouds?

Having children, biologically or spiritually, brings us closer to God. Long before our first baby's birth, I began to *feel* vital to my baby's life. It was like a prophesy. It was also during that pregnancy that I clearly felt the need for nearness to God, yet I'd never been baptized in any church. This need led me to baptism when I was seven months pregnant. The link between mothers and children is more than a one-way street. We are not altogether the teachers and they the pupils.

If we feel put-upon and trapped by our motherhood, it's only because we are not seeing the rainbow. We have as much to gain, to learn from our children as we have to give. Our babies not only teach us how to love God. Ours also taught me how to laugh at myself, and I never could have, without the growing Mary-like certainty inside that the good God who had got us all into this was right there with me every step of the way. Knowing he's near makes it easy to laugh and to teach our children the joy they first bubbled with before we discouraged it with adult doubts and fears.

Peace and good humor have to be very close—and both come to us unsullied and innocent in our babies, who are willing to love so freely. It's no small thing to cherish this part of them, for it's very close and dear to God. More—in protecting them in this, we too are touched and drawn nearer to our balance and our God.

I can't imagine a Christ who provided more wine for a wedding feast, who did not also bring good humor along with him. But good humor is more than a silly giggle. It's the chuckle that's so deep inside we may not even let it out. Strange, isn't it, that we're usually laughing at ourselves and the pickles we get into. Take away the pickle and there is no laugh.

Sure, a family's physical needs are always dunning us and they are important. But youngsters need more than to be washed and clothed and fed. They need a mother so sure of God's abiding love that she's not afraid of appearing absurd.

Husbands, like children, seem to have an aversion to being made the butt of jokes, but that isn't the big reason it's up to mom to learn to be the buffoon. It's because she is the barometer whose disposition shows whether there is sunshine or storms ahead for the whole family.

That doesn't mean we need to stifle all those liberated ideas. It means that, no matter how liberated we are or want to be, there are responsibilities that go even with liberation, and one of these is that we are the core of our family's ability to love. All of their future relationships with others and with God are built on how *we* love. Liberation helps us take this role seriously. It takes a very cool, self-contained personality to be able to laugh at herself. That's why so many women curdle instead, and so do their families.

Only—life is too short and too serious for us to keep looking at the clouds. Besides, there's always a rainbow *somewhere,* and the kids need to learn how to peek around the fog and into the lights and colors and promise of it. Humor is the light that points the way to hope.

My mother used to tell us, "when you get up feeling grumpy, *make* yourself sing a song. Better yet, a silly song. Before you're halfway through, everything will look brighter."

And, you know, *it does.*

Poking fun at yourself also makes everyone else immediately feel better. Sure, your ego will suffer, but then what else *is* Christian humility but the absence of an inflated ego? In most cases, egos being the tough little monsters they are, they can stand periodic puncturing anyway. The first time you try this it will hurt, so start easy by just letting your faults show through.

Take the day that begins with a roar and food is diminished at breakfast in a splintered second.

"How did they *do* it?" Dad gasps. "All that oatmeal! And that was *fifteen* eggs!"

This is *not* the time to brag about your cooking. Anyway, you and I both know a kid would eat the knot off a log, given a chance. It's time to pat that new matronly bulge beginning to form at your waist and say, "Maybe they just enjoy food like I do."

You can lick your wounds when they're at school, dad's working, and you feel like a sieve through which questions have been poured and answers expected automatically to drip out. Have another egg and piece of toast with strawberry jam, or you *can* be a martyr and have some black coffee.

Just getting the kids ready for breakfast can give your ego a beating. *Why* do all boys put their undershirts on backwards and never tuck in their shirttails? *Why* do little girls lose their socks and panties and petticoats and skirts and hair ribbons and anything else that belongs in their dressers?

When at last you're alone with the babies, you look around the teen-age daughter's room and one of the many problems of the day leaps at you. Decision. Do you stoop over from now until lunchtime picking up and putting away? Or close the door on the whole mess and expect daughter to put everything in its place when she comes in?

SLOTH IS A SIN! This fine statement should be tacked on the bulletin board in every home. Meanwhile, this room and this mess are *hers*. Let her clean them up.

The later decisions in favor of kids helping erase their morning tracks when they come home seem right—until the onslaught.

"It isn't my job! It's hers."

"*She* dropped the papers on the rug!"

"Baby spilled the ashtray! I didn't!"

"You said I wouldn't have to do dishes after six months. It's not my job anymore!"

Yes, sloth is a sin. But for whom? If any daughter of ours wants to live in an untidy slum and provided she's over twelve and ought to know better, I let her have it.

One of our girls, thus allowed to follow the path of half-eaten apples and strung-around clothes, for some unfathomable reason fell in love with and married a neat-as-a-pin young man. I *so* wanted to warn him, but decided to butt out. How would this early infringement upon their judgment be taken from an almost-mother-in-law? Besides, love is blind and nobody would have listened.

But it wasn't two weeks until she was back, sniffing around home again. This time she watched closely *and learned* the fine art of cleanliness and neatness she hadn't considered worthy of her time the first go-round.

So much for sloth, at least where young people are concerned. Husbands are something else. If you're lucky and have the kind of man who slings his dirty socks under the bed, *this is not a fault!* Husbands do us favors like this so we can get down on our knees and say our morning prayers. Only for heaven's sake, don't forget to pick up the socks. They smell.

If your husband's the kind who takes off gardening clothes and drops them, complete with peat moss and fertilizer, onto your cedar chest, *don't nag!* Nagging, they say, is a woman's worst fault. I never nag, though I do scream a little on occasion. A man's house may be his castle, but does that mean it has to be my slum?

Actually, women's liberation to the contrary, I see no reason at all for not putting every feminine wile known to me to use, to get my husband to keep up his end by hanging up his clothes and picking up his papers. If this makes me a sex object, is that bad? There are times to be liberated and times to make your man feel ten feet tall so he can be liberated too.

In any marriage, there is no such thing as *one* liberated person. Either one is the master, the other the slave, or one trying to break the bonds and the other feeling threatened, or each allowing the other to be free. A woman's attitude often makes the man's attitude what it is. Why not help him to grow? You'll both feel better that way.

Likewise, the mother's approach to her children makes all the difference in the world in how they behave. If you begin the morning by telling the kids how naughty they are, *within the hour* you will have mother-produced fireworks, litter, and mayhem.

There's more than one way to keep a house clean, and I prefer to do it so all the backbending is not mine. It depends totally on how one starts the day. I try to begin the day by telling the kids how helpful, neat, and quiet they are. Well, maybe *quiet* is stretching even a psychological point. But before the day's over, they're shining their halos like crazy and the house has somehow become over half clean, which is a very good average for our family.

The same approach works when you want a day off. Without forethought, your momentary flight from home can become all tears, gulps, and clinging. The one and only way to leave children and have a pleasant memory to hold to while you're gone, is to give the baby-sitter a chance! If a child clings to your skirt and whines and cries for you, her dependency can be so appealing many mothers take it for all the ego boost they can get out of it and use this unfortunate moment to hug and love the child.

Result: The child, who *would* have been happy after you'd gone, presents the sitter with immediate problems that it may take an hour to settle. You, on the other hand, though your ego has been given a lift, can't help but remember the doleful eyes and pitiful begging of those greatest con artists in the world—small children. Is that *really* the way to begin a nice afternoon's or evening's entertainment?

We always preferred to tell the kids, well before we left, that we were going *and would be coming back.* When? We always left that hazy, because more mayhem can come about if the kid can tell time and something delays you. All they have to know is that they're to behave, *and that you're coming back.* With all of that once said, we left as soon as the baby-sitter arrived. That way the con artists didn't have time to set up their pitches. Result: We saw them smiling and waving as we drove off and nothing could possibly go wrong. Of course, our kids are not all that angelic, but the system works as often as most family systems do where there are constant and often premeditated breakdowns in communication.

Speaking of angels, it was an awful jolt the first time I read that, to their children, a mother and father represent God. But surely this means, too, that too much worry and prim dignity that overwhelms children can produce an unreal and unfortunate distance later between them and God.

Anyway, I can't believe the Christ who picked up little children in his arms and played with them told them sober theological facts. He knew them, so he must have known they wouldn't love him so well if he didn't laugh, teach, and play with them all at the same time.

Dignity isn't worth much unless you're applying for a job or a loan at the bank or are entertaining your boss's wife. I know that kids prefer a mother willing to do an Irish jig or a fleahop in the kitchen while the pancakes are browning. Such a sight freezes the fighting right out of the small fry. Then they turn to giggles. And before long, out of this nonsense they come to the idea mothers spend their lives trying to *tell* them. That all saints are happy saints, and why not give it a whirl?

This does not imply that I or other mothers are necessarily saints, even the Mary-Martha mothers. We're only trying to be. I know what they say on Mother's Day cards and so do you, but don't you believe it! Falling for her own publicity only makes a woman insufferably proud or insufferably guilty. Alone, we have but a faint flicker of saintliness. Always and always, we require our Lord every step of the way.

A woman who knows she belongs to the mystical Body of Christ shouldn't be afraid of a little silliness. Nor afraid to sing even when she's off-key and her kids are like mine and plug their ears and stare as if they can't believe this horror. All of this makes them feel very important, and when we are unafraid of being ourselves around them, the family warmth deepens.

It's beautiful, being loved by your family. When mom is joyous and unafraid, so are the small fry in household things and in family living. It will also make them unafraid as they reach for spiritual ties.

A Martha too often is stolid, serious, and busy. Too busy to goof off. Being both a Mary and a Martha, we still get things done, but we're never too busy for a little joy along the way. When you hold God in your heart long enough, love for him deepens and so does your prayer. Soon, then, you begin to feel that surge of pure joy that flows up from within resources you didn't know you had. For that matter, you didn't have them. They're called graces—and they come only when called upon.

Family life would have gone out of fashion eons ago if there were no spurts of gaiety and laughter to help us over the bumps. And maybe it's the godless lack of hope and joy in too many worldly homes today that has brought the family unit to its present shaky status. Who wants to get involved in love relationships that hold no joy?

But the Christian home has built-in sources of joy— mothers filled with the graces of their vocation and who believe Christ meant it when he said, "As the Father has loved me, so have I loved you, abide in my love. If you keep my commandments, you will abide in my love, just as I have kept my Father's commandments, and abide in his love. These things I have spoken to you, that my joy may be in you and that your joy may be full" (John 15:9-11). Such comforting words to remember, to clutch desperately during family crises.

Already the day begins gee-hawed, when you find you're out of peanut butter for lunches, four kids missed the school bus, the washer is broken down, and the last diaper is on the baby.

That's the bad news.

Maybe the good news is that you learn by good old on-the-job training that sandwiches can also be made from other things. Dill pickles, raspberry jam, honey-butter, or any of the other combinations that usually spice up plain peanut butter. They can nourish, too. Besides, today's the day to recall that peanut butter sticks to teeth and causes cavities when the kids are sloppy about brushing.

Allow me to warn you, though, there may be repercussions.

Our most meticulous boy, on such a day, slipped away without his abnormal sandwich which had breached the peanut-butter-geared customs of our family—and came home that night gloating over the other kids. *His* teacher had paid for a hot lunch for him after he'd shown her the lone cold pancake he'd taken along to tide him over!

On such a day, it's nine-thirty before you're through chauffering kids to school and the baby *has* to be wet. Should this throw you?

Certainly not. You may find a good use for old dish towels right there. And old receiving blankets later. And if the service man is too late, even old sheets. But don't let the service man know you've managed. You probably needn't worry about this if you have more than five children. It's likely your utility room stays filled with dirty clothes and the very sight of the untidy mountain will stick like a burr in his memory to the good advantage that the next time you have trouble, he'll be out on the double.

So it's one-thirty before you manage to nibble a short lunch. Even on such a day, *especially* on such a day, it's vital to your faith, to yourself, and to the family's sanity that you stop and evaluate. Are you a frazzled Martha, or is there a Mary aching inside of you to get out?

Keep that balance! Even if it's a day so far askew that the kids refuse to shut their eyes for naps, you can shut their door and rise above them with a half hour's spiritual reading. Read the holy Bible so slowly and quietly aloud that you can actually taste the words on your lips, and they will seep tranquillity into your soul. This is God talking directly to you. Taste and enjoy.

And gather strength for the dinner hour.

7

TV—A Controllable Power

While we seek actively to keep our Mary-Martha balance, to keep our relationship with God real and relaxed, we dare not forget that for the first time in history, family homes have an outside teacher on the premises with more one-to-one influence on our youngsters than even we mothers have. It's this teacher that has convinced so many mothers that fleeing their homes is more fulfilling than loving where it counts. And why not? Few intelligent women wish to be identified with the morons who whine and simper in helpless confusion before simple choices like detergents or toothpastes.

TV, of course. A marvelous teacher, but a dangerous one on two counts besides what it's done to you and me. It's always entertaining to our children, as you and I can't possibly be for every waking moment. With rare exception, it says or shows or teaches nothing about the goodness, the mercy, and the tremendous love of our Lord.

Such a setup takes consistent awareness from mom, both to fill in the gaps and to offset the great clots of violence and offensiveness that also come through the advertisements of shows we may not even watch or commercials we can't help watching. Never mind the responsibility; the networks have to clean themselves up. We know it and they know it, but if we waited for the greedy world to clean itself up before having children, Adam and Eve would never have had Cain and Abel.

It's our duty, yours and mine, to *react* when our families are confronted with values alien to our own. We went through a real crisis as a result of TV violence which had not yet been proven, as it now has, to have disastrous influence on children.

TV had a stranglehold on our family. We were willing victims of an infatuation which swept us along a sluggish current of happy do-nothingness. Then our three-year-old became suddenly subjected to a fire-setting, bear-killing, man-shooting violence in his talk and dreams that were not bettered by any of the answers which had calmed our other children.

True, we had a new baby and he was probably angry with his world. But none of the others had suffered this severely from sibling jealousy. All previous experience, all sought advice failed—until our TV set broke down!

Then, with a suddenness verging on the miraculous, his fury resolved and our family's equilibrium righted itself. At last the efforts we had been making for our son could make themselves felt. There *had* to be some connection between the violence which even our selected family programs contained at times and his anger at the world showing itself in such violent forms.

Until that time, we had sat happily like fifteen sponges, sopping up what others desired us to think and learn—until we had all but lost the blessed faculty of thinking for ourselves. We had become totally oblivious to a growing dissension among our older children. Not the loud, noisy, obvious kind which follows perfectly healthy children in perfectly healthy fights, but something subtler and more disastrous. A lack of *ties* of the common family variety, shared experiences which do so much to teach youngsters to live at peace with themselves.

All the tremendous good TV has to offer, we had been wasting. Without realizing it, we had let slip the very moorings upon which such an entertaining medium of education may best be used. Our mistake was simple and almost universal. We were seeing too much too often.

Our family has always preferred quality to quantity. But with TV's many channels, there are almost always educational, highly entertaining programs with the just-right features of a fair family show. It sneaked up on us. We had thought, those first years, that educational programs good enough for the children were the all-important thing. Alas, it is not so. Too much of anything is gluttony and ours is becoming a nation of TV gluttons.

Can such an attitude be good even for the sponsors of TV shows? How much attention do they really receive from a hypnotized zombie? At our house, when the noise was over and the "Star Spangled Banner" proclaimed the end of another old, old show, there would be a heavy sigh—and not one more thought given to the show or who sponsored it. Just an immense relief that the great one-eyed hypnotist was silent at last and we were released from eye-reddened bondage until another day.

Now we have developed, at last, a little of the thing called self-control. A great accomplishment when you have floundered in the whirling depths of TV madness as we had.

A mild awakening came one night at PTA when one of the parents asked the teacher, "How do you get the child away from the TV set long enough to get his homework done?"

The teacher fumbled for an answer and came up with, "I don't know. We have the same trouble with our boy. We like TV, too, so why shouldn't our children enjoy it?"

But she still didn't offer a solution for the homework.

There is a saying—practice what you preach. When parents absorb with fascination, their children can be expected to do likewise. We tried to change this little rule, but it didn't work.

Our eldest daughter was the dishwasher. And dishes and TV don't mix if you value clean dishes. Her mind would sing along with the latest idol swaying on the screen in the living room, while she tapped her foot and kept time at the sink— and tiptoed in to watch at least forty times per program.

What was worse, Bill and I were too absorbed to see. We were seeing everything at half-mast those days. Even at meal times we were almost too foggy to notice the condition of the dishes.

As for the unlimited educational programs, we're still all for them—for somebody else's children. For ourselves, we love too well the bright-eyed, self-thinking children who came back to us after they'd had time to develop their own initiative. Think what would happen to children, even in the most excellent schools, if they were expected to attend them every waking minute. Educational TV must have a place and it's a pity it isn't used more in schools where its tremendous power to teach would carry such an advantage.

As for us, we simply cannot have it in such huge doses in our home. We deeply feel that the Christian home is a training school where the teachers are loving parents. Where the children are shown, through love, cooperation, *and example*, the proper way to become discerning, moral adults.

I was all set one night, in the middle of our best TV program, with a four-decker sandwich and a bottle of cold Coke when I stopped to take a good look at myself. Was *this* unthinking vegetable what I wanted our children to become?

My feeble attempts at self-control were bolstered when our set broke down.

And we are all humbly grateful. One full evening passed and not *one* child raised a voice so loud it could be heard above a TV commercial. We really *saw* our ten-year-old, rosy and pajamaed, for the first time since we had placed the TV in our home, when she said at bedtime, "I wish we never would get that TV back. It's been so nice and peaceful tonight."

Bill and I had thought that first night pretty rugged. My mind felt rudderless. I'm sure it was. There hadn't been an original thought in years. My husband and I, who had always had so much to say to each other, had become listless and tongue-tied.

The next night we fared a little better. Someone found the checkers again, another hauled out the jigsaw puzzle from our Christmas box and the teen-agers happily made fudge while I read a bedtime story to the toddlers—and could not remember how long it had been since I had turned them over to the TV. Only then did I realize what we had been doing to our family.

A child must learn, above all, to think and discern for himself. We think he won't be able to do this if he is over-exposed to stories, music, programs which are spoonfed from someone else's laboratory of how to live. We hold that a mother's sacred trust as well as her God-given right is to select, guide, and train her child along the ways best suited for that child as a unique person.

It follows, then, that we must not only carefully select his/her TV diet but also thoughtfully curtail it when necessary. It's far too easy for kids to learn to spout what they have seen, parrotlike, without exercising their own individual interpretation or judgment.

We have seen, through our thirteen youngsters, that young minds sharpen and grow with *interchange* of ideas—evaluating, accepting, or rejecting. We talk in normal tones now, instead of the TV-stimulated screech that reaches over commercials. We don't race madly over sprawled feet, shoving arms and legs away in our haste to grab a box of crackers from the cupboard and a dish of salad from the refrigerator, and rush back to the living room to sink into the easy chair before the program begins again.

We have likened our awakening to the nights we have let our babies "cry it out." With TV, as with babies, there came the inevitable night when one of us wanted to give in and "just enjoy it." We still have our weak moments with TV. But so far there has been one or the other still capable of getting up and turning the knob.

For there are definite compensations in limited televiewing. With sharpened awareness to the life around us, our family is far more eager each evening to enjoy quietly the one program which we allow ourselves. We plan each week in advance to ensure a well-balanced program for the benefit of all.

Sponsors please note, we are enjoying every minute of your commercials now. The rapt attention they command would warm any businessman's heart. And it's honest, *thinking* interest, the kind that brings the tune back to mind while we're shopping.

We have rediscovered that a lively discussion with friends is a fine way to spend an evening. An enthusiastic family dialogue takes over now during dinner, dialogue that ranges from world peace to sex to religion, and even the last is two-way, four-way, and very open.

We had thought our teen-agers would object to our new arrangement. Instead they were delighted to entertain us with the top ten records. We are a family doing things together.

We read more. I'm catching up on that long list of books I meant to read years ago. My husband is catching up on a long list of household jobs that keep him reminded he is a happy husband and I am a caring wife. Our grocery bill is shrinking, along with our waistlines and my own "TV spread."

Weekends we have no TV at all, since that's our family time. We've at last faced it—there are always indispensable programs. We now treat TV as a welcome *invited* guest in our home. Not here to rob us and drug us, to throw our children into nightmares and cause awkward silences between marriage partners. But a guest well respected because of his tremendous power.

Our children are not keeping up on *all* the latest on TV. But now we're very sure they're keeping up on the things we want them to know. How to get along as witnesses for Christ in a world where so many people regrettably have lost contact with each other through the spoon-feeding to which they subject themselves, via overdoses of TV.

Now *I* have more time to do what *I* want occasionally "just because." I am a better woman for it, and we are a better family. There's even time to pray both with the family and alone. It has given me, given *all* of us, a Christ-centered balance again.

8

Shared Family Prayer

One of our teen-agers showed me how much our offspring rely on what they see. He had gone off to college and came back filled with fervor for the reading of the Holy Bible. He stopped in midsentence to look squarely at me.

"Mom, why don't *you* ever try reading it? *Our* Bible just sits there for show." He pointed to the big picture Bible on the book case.

"I do read it," I answered. "I just didn't think I had to read it in front of everybody. My Bible's by my bed. The one on this stand is beautiful, but it's too heavy to hold." I felt my face flush in annoyance and in sudden painful realization. Because I'd valued the peace and quiet as I read the Scripture passages, I hadn't understood I was cheating our kids of *their* share of inspiration. I should have shared at least some of it!

The importance of sharing can be there in almost any kind of prayer meaningful to your family. Each church, each community in Christ, has avenues of prayer suitable for family use. These range from booklets such as *The Upper Room*, *The Secret Room*, and *These Days* to the rosary, one of the family prayers of the Catholic. But I'd been too busy a Martha keeping house. Today I know this *alone* will always keep a woman too occupied for extra prayers. Likely too, her concentration on house will cause a rising resentment in her at the distraction of a child's chatter.

Also, to be a Mary you have to realize your youngsters are learning far more than you suppose, *in the very memories of you* that are being printed on the tapes of their minds. Ours will always remember that their family offered its family prayers in remembrance of deceased relatives and friends, in petition for those in trouble, in thanksgiving for the gifts we have received from God. Someday your children will look back and know that your prayers together as a family have shaped their earliest memories *and* their lives.

Devotion to prayer seems to have fallen into disuse among many Christian families and I can't imagine why. Oh, we hear many ordinary excuses that add up to the Martha's "anxious and troubled about many things," and it *is* easy to let a spiritual exercise that loses meaning for you get squeezed out.

It isn't important what spiritual exercise a family uses, so long as its members try to do some praying together. The one most important privilege open to Christian mothers (and fathers) is the building of strong habits of shared family prayer that cement family unity. You know the old saying about a chain's weakest link. *We* think the weakest link in habits of prayer are the beginnings, the puttings off. Habit can only be as strong, too, as the youth and persistence of its beginning. *Very* early is about right.

Way back during World War II, Bill and I worked in a shipyard on graveyard shift nights and ran an eighty-acre farm days because Bill was too old for the draft. I managed four hours of sleep per day and Bill only two, so from sheer fatigue, religion began to take a back seat. We were even too tired to realize it had. We had only two children then.

We felt that church attendance was becoming a terrible stumbling block in our weekends. Still we went doggedly every Sunday as obliged, but sat there beside our children like two wooden Indians, trying desperately to keep each other awake and not hearing the sermon, too exhausted to participate at all.

After several such Sundays and wearied of the effort, I said, "Bill, this is ridiculous. We're doing nobody any good when we can't stay awake enough to hear or see or share in what's going on. Let's talk to the pastor about it."

We went to the rectory and explained. "*Must* we go through these empty motions?" I pleaded.

"Do you have any children?"

"Yes, two. They're out in the car."

"How old are they?"

"Three and five."

He smiled gently at us then and said, "I know how hard it must be on you. But children of three and five are old enough to remember very well. If *I* were you, I'd come for their sakes. *You want a child's first memories to be of the family's coming to church on Sundays.*"

We thanked him and left, a bit disgusted as I remember. But the truth of his words kept needling us and finally we had to admit he was right. He had known *exactly* what we wanted for our children. The only way children learn to love God is through loving parents who show their devotion *in ways a child can see.* Children believe what they see.

I became much more insistent on our children behaving, after I realized the two-year-old had memorized and could mimic the beer commercials on TV. That told me she was old enough to learn to pray. Even before the little ones are old enough to *say* prayers, I keep whispering when they get restless during prayer, "Just think about how God loves you."

We don't give enough credit to a child's capacity to love. Long before most of us are aware of it, a small child is ready for mental prayer. If we'd let him, he could teach us a thing or two about meditating, too. Remember the definition for prayer—raising your mind and heart to God? This is what we, as Mary-Marthas, are teaching when we show the very small child he can think of God just as the rest of the family does when they pray.

Unfortunately, many husbands are not as agreeable to family prayers as their wives, and my husband was no exception. But I didn't press the matter. Shared family prayer is something parents don't argue over. Men and women are meant to complement each other, after all.

Mothers have always been the first to begin customs that teach things of moral values and we still are, no matter how liberated we become. From what I've seen, the mother usually takes the lead in gathering the brood together to say these prayers, even in households where the father, once cured of his reluctance, comes later to lead them.

Our family was half grown and still Bill always heaved a big sigh and complained as prayer time drew near, "I'm too tired to kneel tonight."

"But you don't have to kneel to pray," I said. "Just sit in that big chair and be comfortable."

"I know, but I still have to fix that leaky faucet." And he was gone in search of tools to fix the dripping of a faucet that had been giving me trouble for weeks.

The next night it was something else. During our prayers, the children's and mine, Bill managed to fix more faucets, trim more hedges, and repair more car damage than in all the other free time he had. Meanwhile I asked the oldest boy to lead us in prayer instead of Bill. This divided prayer pattern repeated itself for several years, until gradually Bill began to feel left out when we all gathered without him.

Slowly he started to join in, maybe once every week or two. Then his construction job came to an end and he was laid off, with no other work in sight. He'd been out of work for weeeks when, one evening, he knelt to pray with us and asked us to pray that he might find another job. The kids took up the chant with fervor and we were on the last decade when the telephone rang and I answered it.

"May I speak to Mr. Hertz?" asked a deep voice.

"Surely."

I called Bill and returned to the family to drop to my knees and finish the prayer with the youngsters. Bill returned in moments, a sheepish but relieved look on his bronzed face. "It was George Wilson. He has a new job for me—and at a dollar over union scale."

"Wow!" I exclaimed. "That's more than you made on your last job."

"Yep. I start tomorrow."

From then on, Bill was with us at prayer every evening.

Our Lord meant it when he said, "Again I say to you, if two of you agree on earth about anything they ask, it will be done for them by my Father in heaven. For where two or three are gathered in my name, there am I in the midst of them" (Matthew 13:19–20). The more our family practiced nearness to him, the dearer became the realization that the protective God who formed and loves and lives within our family is really present with it each evening for the few minutes the prayer requires.

There is no more effective way of building a rope of faith around your family than by weaving it every evening, strand by strand, with shared family prayers, until a rope of strength is formed that will bind you together as no other form of prayer can do. And is there any good reason why such prayer cannot follow the reading of Sacred Scripture?

Yet—we treasure our quiet times alone, and we should. But when a mother allows herself to become pregnant, she invites others to join her. Each of us wants to, and should, meditate and pray. But *not* if we sacrifice the faith of our youngsters to do it. God has entrusted these little ones to our care. It simply is not true that if it *feels* that way, you *are* closer to God when praying alone than when you're teaching his little ones how to love him and pray to him.

Being a mother can't ever quite be the same as being a Mary, a contemplative. We were meant to be Mary-Marthas, whose work and distractions *are* our prayers. Earthly clamor is the music of our souls even when it sounds to us like the rasping of a fingernail against a blackboard. Only by living it and guiding the children and enduring, if necessary, can we hope to grow as mothers, yes, but in our own selfhood too. Motherhood is a solid and meaning-filled vocation that develops us, body and soul, as women, not just an accident of nature, an avocation, as some have declared and others have made of it. The "working mother," or more accurately the one who gets paid in legal tender for her work, cannot shuck her responsibility to her children just because she "works out," any more than can the homemaker who "works in." Either can be an excellent mother. Either can fail miserably. It's how much you care and give of yourself and your faith that counts.

A mother's *emotional* faith is a beautiful thing, but emotion is elusive and deceptive. We have to be alert to its pitfalls. *Quiet and aloneness can so terribly easily become shallow escape from the life which is really ours.*

Take peace and quiet, for instance. They're fine—if you can get them. *I've* seldom been so lucky. If I'd waited for quiet before I prayed, I'd never have begun. Moreover, neither would our children, *because I would not have shown them how.* This way, no matter how great my faults, at least I've been able to point them into the right paths. What they do with it as they grow up is up to them and their free wills.

But before you can let your light shine before others, you have to light it. The rosary, like other forms of family prayer, is first and forever an open invitation, a guiding light to meditation, discussion, and Scripture reading on the life and passion, the holy example of our Lord.

As our family began to see small miracles happening as a result of our prayers for others, we were all encouraged. Our middle children (eight to twelve) found it more interesting to offer their prayers especially for someone who badly needed God's help. Eagerly, then, they watched for the changes to take place as a result of our prayers.

One evening I suggested we all pray for a family whose parents had not been to church for fifteen years. We were to keep it up for a full year before the father, apparently "for no good reason," decided to go to church! Two months later the mother joined him and shortly after that their two children, the same ages as our middle ones, were baptized.

The resulting enthusiasm at our house didn't let up for weeks. We prayed up a storm. We went on to include another friend whose husband would permit no religious discussion or religion of any sort in his home, though his wife was a Christian. It's still too soon for results, but the mighty power of the prayers of the innocent can't but ease an unhappy situation.

We don't hold a stopwatch on how long it takes a prayer or series of them to bring results. You could get very shaken if you couldn't *see* a change that may long ago have taken place in another's heart. Our prayers, I think, simply place the problems, with a reminder, back into God's lap. He will take them from there.

One of our daughters used to resist and fuss when she had to join us in prayer. Night after night her face clearly portrayed her suffering. Her mouth pulled down, her voice whined, her shoulders slumped. She could have won a dramatics contest. Furthermore, it almost worked. For years she *almost* had me convinced I might be wrong in "forcing" her to pray with the rest of us.

She was seventeen when she quit school before graduation to marry a boy who was also a high school dropout. They drove to another state where a seasonal job as laborer beckoned, leaving his parents and Bill and me shocked and disappointed. His, because the boy had not finished high school. We, over her lack of schooling and because they'd been married by a justice of the peace, not in church. They were gone from home six months and all we heard from them were phone calls and occasional letters. I prayed and worried over her.

But when she came back, almost her first words were, "You didn't need to worry about us, mom. I've done a lot of nutty things, I guess. But all the time, you just better believe I always remembered my prayers!" With her words, hope began to rise in me again, and eight years later they were married in the church.

Shared family prayers show our children how to easily open the door to mental prayer and meditation on our Lord's passion. The depths of the mystery are limitless, just as these thoughts I share with you are but a tiny scratch on the surface of the meditations you can teach your family.

As your own growth as a Mary-Martha mother gradually comes more easily, so will your insight into the spiritual needs of your little ones. Your family prayers, when keeping pace with your growth as a person of equality with your family, can only make you a better, more loving wife and mother.

You will not be the only one who grows. For love is boundless where free choice and responsibility unite. And love becomes a rising tide that cannot be stopped until it overflows to the children entrusted to your care by the God of whom you are a very part.

9

Special Children
Can Teach Us

One of the most important areas of learning we need to teach
our children is how to be compassionate. Sometimes I think
only the very poor or the very rich learn it, for the poor can
not be threatened more and the rich have nothing to fear of
giving because it won't hurt anyway.

We've become a nation of many Marthas whose example
in materialism is rapidly soaked up by our children and
transferred by time and growth and education into a
selfishness that leaves no room for any cares but that of self.
Self-worship has lately reached the point of idolatry.

Though it's laying a heavy burden on mothers, I really do
feel that society will not make an about-face *until the
mothers show their children that money is not what counts,
but love.* Mostly we're too busy and too concerned over tight
budgets to let shine through what love we harbor beneath the
surface. Like all else, this attitude is not taught but caught. *It
isn't what we say, but what we do that tells our youngsters
where our values are.*

Like other mothers who are in business as well as having
children at home to care for, I had not realized how much
had gone undone in the training of our youngsters until out-

side influences showed me the truth. Hindsight is so accurate!

Larry, then a sixth-grader, came home from school one day in the fall with a soft glow of tenderness on his face—a look altogether out of character for the rough-and-tumble, loud-talking, foot-stamping child he was.

"Mom, you know what?" His voice held an urgency he was eager to share. "I kept a blind girl from getting hit by a swing today!" His face beamed with pride.

"Yes, Mommy," Brian, the fourth-grader, added. "She's a first-grader and she walks around the school grounds with the rest of us. *But she's blind!*" A very real charity was obvious as this talkative, careless son of ours went on. "I gave her *my* swing, and she had lots of fun. And I watched her, too, to make sure she didn't go too high or get hurt. You know what? You have to be careful with the special education kids, 'cause they can't play just like the rest of us. Lots of special education kids have to try real hard to do what we can do easy."

"You know," Larry said, "there's a girl who comes from right close to here. She talks kind of slow and acts kind of funny sometimes. But we *never* make fun of her!"

"*'Course not!*" Brian was so emphatic I couldn't believe my ears. "She can't help it. And besides," his voice carried heaven-sent wisdom, "if we're careful with her, maybe she'll be able to play as good as us someday."

We had tried to teach the youngsters to be kind and understanding toward others, but obviously experience is the best teacher. The experience came about as a result of the unique school situation in that city, which integrated into the public schools the pupils enrolled in special education classes. It had developed a progressive program for handicapped children.

I was so overwhelmed by the new insight, new understanding and consideration for others which my children were gaining that I sought out the man in charge of the special education group. I wanted to see for myself whether this setup was as good for the handicapped youngsters as it had been for our normal ones.

The director explained to me that a new wing, barely completed, was an important part of our children's elementary school. This wing was given over to the special classes for exceptional children and was continually in the process of improvement. The blind, for example, had a wealth of Braille books as well as Braille typewriters. Partially blind pupils learned regular typing in the same wing.

They also had a supply of special boards to help blind students learn to write script. These resembled clipboards but had a soft rubber base covered by an acetate sheet, which was written upon with a special ball-point pen. On these colorless sheets, writing and pictures left deep grooves that formed patterns for fingers to trace—trees, landscapes, script. The children learned geography by touch, too, from the many relief maps in the wing.

The special education staff included twenty-two people who provided not only classroom teaching but psychological and psychometric services and other services especially needed by children with speech, hearing, and vision defects.

The director was enthusiastic about the development and progress of his system, but said, "There is constant and continued need for cooperation between the home and the school. The home can be particularly helpful in encouraging the acceptance of exceptional children in the schools."

Many parents, he claimed, didn't seem to understand the advantages their own children could gain from daily association with handicapped classmates. Yet daily we saw that *ours* were getting lessons in compassion and courage, consideration for others, and unselfishness.

We're often told that crippled or otherwise exceptional

children are made unhappy by being treated as "different." Yet I found that children seem to value differences. Even kindergartners love to bring to school anything they may have that is different and of interest to the others—a new record, a new turtle, perhaps a new hearing aid.

There was great excitement in our children's kindergarten one morning when a little cerebral-palsied child, who also had hearing impairment, displayed her hearing aid. The children all wanted to try it out for themselves. And can't you imagine one of these youngsters, years later, upon learning about his own impending deafness, recalling with a smile—not the fear that is common—the experiments with the hearing aid?

The teacher that day took advantage of the children's interest. She not only explained the little girl's hearing aid, but also told the story of how she had been afflicted. The youngsters were fascinated.

Two days later the child's mother received a phone call from a neighbor. "Can my Peggy come over and play with your little girl for a while? She'd just love to, if it's all right with you."

As the girl's mother told me about the call her lips trembled. "That was the first time in our daughter's seven years of life that *anyone* ever asked to play with her. I agreed, of course, but I couldn't help asking why."

And the neighbor had answered, "Well, you see, Peggy goes to kindergarten with your daughter and the teacher explained how she'd been hurt when she was born—and, to tell you the truth, Peggy knows more about it than I do."

And so understanding brought about a friendship valuable to both children. I told the mother our children had profited in much the same way.

She replied, "Not everybody feels as you do about school."

"What do you mean?"

She looked thoughtful before she answered, and when she did, her heart was showing. "I happened to be in the classroom one day when a mother of one of the normal children came in to speak with the teacher. I don't think she knew who I was, but she pointed to our daughter and asked the teacher, 'My child won't have to be in the same room with *that*, will she?' "

I didn't know what to say, so I glanced toward the little girl. She was happily and quietly playing with her doll on the floor. She had dressed it and was trying to tie a bow at the back of the tiny dress, struggling persistently with muscles that refused to respond. She caught me watching her, ducked her head, then smiled up at me shyly.

Any Mary-Martha would have been touched. I silently thanked God that we lived in a city that offered our youngsters this wonderful opportunity to learn about and know other exceptional human beings. Their new understanding was helping them to find the *person* beneath the differences, whether those differences were fleeting, like a broken arm, or more lasting, such as blindness, deafness, or cerebral palsy.

According to the kindergarten teacher, the child with cerebral palsy had never been a problem. "The other children feel privileged to help her when she needs help, as with her wraps or boots."

The girl's mother was equally emphatic. "I'm so thankful she's allowed to attend school with normal children! It's helped her in every possible way."

The child attended regular school for half of each day and special education classes for the other half. I asked the director of the program if he thought institutions for special children were on their way out.

"No, unfortunately," he replied. "The institutions do have a place. But as far as possible they'd *like* to put themselves out of business. Ultimately, I think most exceptional children will take part in the regular school programs."

We both knew, of course, that this will only come with public acceptance of parents, and that there will always be a small percentage of exceptional children who must have institutional care.

I asked the mother of two deaf children what she thought of having her youngsters in a regular school. Since this was their first year, she was reluctant to give an opinion. "It's really too soon to tell, but I *can* say this. Here, they're delighted to go to school. Before, when we took them to the school for the deaf two hundred miles away, they'd cling to me and beg us not to send them away from home. The deaf school's a fine one," she added hastily, "but the kids are just too young to be so far from home. Now finally they can enjoy a normal family life and the companionship of normal children. More than anything else," her words slowed, "I want my two deaf children to learn that the world is theirs, too, as much as it is yours and mine. In regular school they are taught lipreading—and they use it. Their classmates give them only one small consideration. That when you talk with a deaf person you should look straight at him and enunciate clearly."

One of the happiest advantages of putting exceptional children into a regular school was that it posed no problem of training facilities. The director said, "If only people could see that the financial burden the schools already carry would not be increased by this system, they could help us in many ways. We're expanding our services to include surrounding communities too small to have their own. Limited as these services must necessarily be, they are far better than placing such children in institutions."

The entire experience of sharing a look into the world of exceptional children as they played and learned with our children made me very sorry that more children could not profit from the system also. Maybe someday . . .

Many parents are unaware that here is a tremendous source for helping their children learn kindness to fellow human beings who have been blessed with less but who, in return, give generously of good nature and cheerfulness *and of hope*.

As parents we all know that what is fostered and allowed to develop will grow. Then why not allow the Mary that lies hidden inside of us think about this marvelous double-sided opportunity for youngsters to learn? Why not foster courage and cooperation? Why not gentleness and compassion? After all, kindness is as contagious as cruelty and we've seen far too much of the latter lately. The way to assure our children a less cruel world is to bring compassion and concern to our own corner of it.

In our city the special education children, as well, *had* to have sensed how important they were in helping others learn the most basic of Christian teachings, "A new commandment I give to you, that you love one another; even as I have loved you, that you also love one another. By this all men will know that you are my disciples, if you have love for one another" (John 13:34–35).

Because "special" children are close to God and good for the formation of our own children, they are close to our hearts also. For the very essence of a Mary is her spiritual love—and where better to exercise it? We Marthas need such lessons as these.

10

The World
through Innocent Eyes

One of the easiest ways to build a faith in our Lord that is fully and clearly open, as a Mary-Martha mother needs to do to find her deepest self, is to see her life through the innocent, unfrantic eyes of the very small child. It may sound moronic to wish to dive into the rabbit hole with Alice to a place where wet spaghetti and a wriggling worm are equally important and fascinating, but it's an experience more weary adults should encounter.

Children have no corner on magic, but the rest of us—we who have been Marthas too long—have all but priced ourselves out of the market of the magical. We've spent ourselves on duty, discipline, and work in such a way that often we've removed from the facts the pleasures and satisfaction they could bring us.

The deadly monotony of the words themselves had formed a cataract over my eyes and attitude that sour day in 1950 when I was no more than a drudging Martha and knew with despair that I'd never been anything else. I *longed* for the peace and quiet of a very lonely mountaintop with every freckle I owned. But there were six children, mountains of laundry, and many miles between me and loneliness.

I brushed my hair out of my eyes and surveyed, through a

curdled disposition, the shambles of the crowded apartment in our modest little motel. I felt drained. I was seven months pregnant and neither my disposition nor my back are at their best in the seventh month. For weeks I had been too depressed to see beyond the confines of our cluttered apartment where six children, the eldest aged ten, intensified everything.

"Larry!" I groaned with a hand pressed into my aching back, "put all those magazines and papers back! You're old enough to know better." I felt like the Old Woman in the Shoe and just wished *I* could spank them all soundly and put them to bed. But if I did they'd only lie there and holler their heads off.

I leaned against the desk and let out a mighty sigh. What was the use? The vacuum cleaner needed emptying. The ironing was heaped from three days ago, but the steam iron weighed a ton. I turned my back on it and headed for the sewing machine and mending. The bobbin was empty. Through blurred eyes I tried to rewind it, and when it fought back and ended in pieces in my hands, I dissolved into tears.

"Mommy, you cwyin'?" Brian's small hand tugged at my skirt as his thumb went back into his mouth and his wide blue eyes became dark with worry.

A rush of guilt made me walk to the bathroom and out of the three-year-old's sight, where I faced the mirror and an unhappy image that bore no resemblance to the carefree woman I longed to be. I stuck my tongue out at it, pushed again at hair that hadn't been put up right for a month—and left the image and the toilet that had been plugged since an hour ago when Peggy had dropped the scissors down it. *Where was that plumber, anyhow?*

The automatic washer droned from the other side of the wall to remind me that even automatics took a lot of stooping. It droned constantly and still I hadn't seen the bottom of the laundry for a week.

I could avoid the dishes no longer. I twisted the spigot and scalding water gushed into the cluttered sink, deflected from an upturned spoon, and splattered onto my hand.

"Ooooh!" I groped for the ointment, then dropped into a chair, sickened by the pain. Everything hurts more when you're tired.

I stared wretchedly at the smudged refrigerator that did *not* defrost itself. Where had the magic gone? I had never expected moonlight and roses. I'd known "for better or for worse" meant I'd also inherited every woman's cleaning problems.

Maybe it was the motel. Seven years before we'd bought—and I'd begun cleaning—an apartment house; and I'd been on the mean end of a mop ever since. Then two years ago Bill began building this motel in eastern Washington— and now each summer we were too busy for a vacation, and each winter we prepared for summer. The children, though I loved every one, had added to the work. Tom, ten, and Janice, seven, were the only two old enough to help when they came home from school.

I was still depressed when Bill arrived at six, as brown and energetic as if taking care of our motel maintenance, doing carpenter work on the side, and being married were all a breeze. He sniffed, lifted the lid on the stew, tasted it, kissed the baby, and then turned to pull me into his arms as an afterthought. I held absolutely still, recognizing my childish self-pity for what it was, but somehow I seemed powerless to rid myself of it.

"Hey! What's wrong with my honey tonight?" He lifted my trembling chin upward and forced me to look at him and suddenly my eyes puddled over and so did the entire horrible day.

Maybe I should have taken those tranquilizers the doctor had wanted to prescribe, but which I'd refused, saying I wanted to face reality. I stole a look into Bill's blue eyes and there was hurt shadowing them. He rocked me against him in silence and then asked, "Dinner ready?"

I nodded and began putting it on the table. Just having an adult around made me feel better. I hadn't known how much I'd missed adult companionship with nothing but infant chatter all day.

After dinner he said suddenly, "Let's go to North Dakota for two weeks and visit Sis. She'd love to see us. Your folks said they'd take care of the motel any time we wanted to get away."

I wasn't so sure. If Barbara and *her* eleven kids had popped in on *me*—I shoved the exhausting thought out and packed. I'd never seen Barbara or her family. Sudden fresh elation filled me. We *could* take the four oldest kids and leave the two smallest with Mom.

By the end of an unbelievable week, we were on our way—and the Chevy was hot and the trip more depressing than I had thought possible. Disaster always results when car and kids refuse to submit to each other. As my enthusiasm wilted more with each passing mile, Bill's expanded.

"Do you realize I haven't been home for sixteen years?" He didn't seem to expect an answer. By now he luxuriated in watching the fields of barley and wheat waltzing in the sweltering prairie winds.

On the third day Janice screeched, "Lookee! Another windmill! And this one's turning! Lookee!" She pointed wildly and all four little faces flattened against the car windows. "And there's a horse!"

"It's Barbara's place, kids. Like it, Jacky?"

I nodded and tried to feel something besides tired. But Barbara—dark, slender, and flushed with pleasure—met us, pulled her apron off, kissed us all, and drew us inside. Adam, thickset and prosperous looking, followed, preceding his eleven goggle-eyed, chattering towheads. When our kids melted into theirs without a ripple and all trooped outside to the horses, my relief was intense.

From then on, we began slipping into another age. Bill had often described it, but I was as unprepared for this life as if I'd been brought here blindfolded. Barbara's eldest daughter scurried through the basement kitchen frying sausages and preparing dinner on a long worktable and the fancy coal range heavy with its full reservoir. I sniffed the spicy smells. This was the summer kitchen while another upstairs was untouched. I couldn't understand this when I saw the upstairs had modern cabinets, an electric refrigerator, and an unused stove.

When I first walked down the hard-packed path toward the outhouse, where the fields spanned out beyond the lazing windmill, the enchantment of the neat buildings and equipment, the cattle and horses, filled me. An incandescent sun shimmered a sultry drowse over the droning flies and I felt a twinge of envy at the blessed peace to be found here away from the burdens of modern "conveniences."

The white-painted outhouse was the most impeccable I'd ever seen. A standard crescent was carved over the door, but the seat inside elegantly sported three holes. And tissue hung so neatly on a modern roller I wished wistfully for an ancient catalogue on a worn string.

As I returned to the house I asked for a drink, which was dipped from a bucket on the worktable and handed me in a long-handled porcelain dipper.

"The windmill pumps the water—as long as there's a wind," Barbara explained. "It only stops three or four days a month."

"How do you get water then?" I felt stupid around farm things.

"We pump it out at the water tank and the boys pump water for the animals. In half an hour apiece the four boys can pump the tank full."

When they had guests, adults were served dinner first at a table as long as a picnic table, while Barbara's youngsters, except the toddler, gaped silently and hungrily from a very close range. But they were so extremely polite and obviously so well trained that I finally relaxed.

Our children had a choice. Tom wrinkled his freckled nose, sniffed the spicy smoked sausages—and elected to sit with the adults. There he bore the disapproving glances of his cousins for all of three bites of sausage before he yielded and slipped away to join them.

Bill was in ecstasy over the borscht, apfelstrudel, and especially the rich-red chokecherry jam, his first since leaving the farm. I was awed by the delicious German potato salad I had never mastered. It was like a postcard from Germany, the entire meal.

Afterward, Barbara proudly showed me her house while Adam led Bill outside to survey the animals and crops. The women returned to the basement and my glance settled again on a bucket set by itself on the floor and almost out of sight. The extreme cleanliness of the place, from cooking to hand-cranking the big milk separator next to the table, made the bucket on the floor even more puzzling. For over an hour it sat untouched and walked-around. Then Barbara's toddler marched over to it, lowered his breeches, and I chuckled aloud. A farm-style potty!

Barbara laughed too. "It saves walking him to the outhouse."

The sun set and lilac shadows crept through the house until my eyes strained to see. Florence struck a match, lit a kerosene lamp, and the shadows receded a little. But the dim light caused the charm of the place to slip a notch, and I was nudged by a feeling I didn't want to identify.

At bedtime, earlier here than Bill and I were used to, Barbara led us upstairs, picking her way ahead of us with the lamp, then holding it aloft for us. She had insisted on bedding our kids down herself and the day lacked but one thing.

"I sure wish I had a bath!" I sighed.

"Oh, I'm sorry I didn't think of it!" Barbara exclaimed. "I'll bring you a basin of water as soon as I can heat it."

"Please, no!" Instant shame plunged me into confusion. "I was only thinking out loud. I didn't mean it."

"Well—if you're sure. But tomorrow's Saturday and we'll all be taking baths then. . . ."

"I'm fine!" I insisted.

Barbara lit the lamp in the bedroom. "It's such a joy to have you!" She beamed at us—and then was gone.

"Boy, what a blunder!" Bill laughed. "Adam's pretty wealthy but only people in town have electricity around here yet. Did you see Barbara's kitchen appliances?"

I nodded. "Too bad they can't use 'em."

"Yeah. Adam bought an electric drill and tomorrow they deliver the electric pump. Adam's so excited you wouldn't believe it! Monday they turn on the lights."

"Really? Barbara said she wasn't sure when. You know, I never realized—." I never finished the sentence. I couldn't explain. It was too vague.

The next day telephone calls poured in from Bill's other relatives and friends, and all carried a sense of mounting excitement. Other farmers around, too, were receiving their first lights. Adam eagerly explained, again and again, details of the forthcoming hookup.

For me, Saturday was one long bath. Barbara heated water on and in the stove and one by one, in a tub by the kitchen, she stripped and scrubbed the unabashed smaller children. As each was finished, she rolled him in a towel and motioned the next into the water. The older ones were left alone to continue the process.

In the late afternoon while I was worrying about the adults' baths, Adam and Bill came in and each was given a basin of warm water to take to his room. Just before supper, Barbara handed me one also—and offered another later for shampooing my hair. Cleanliness could be a lot of work and I saw, too clearly, how very far one small pan of water will stretch.

Sunday evaporated in an acceleration of church, hospitality, and neighbors, while Barbara and her daughters produced, as if by magic, a gigantic ham dinner.

The awaited Monday morning burst over the farmhouse, and while the children churned through their chores, Adam paced the floor waiting for the meter man and a new freezer that came and was set up.

Barbara's cheeks shone a pretty pink. "I can hardly wait to pack away those heavy sadirons!" she rhapsodized. "So I can breeze through the ironing with a light iron. And just think! I'll *really* be washing with an automatic washing machine instead of that wringer gasoline model that takes all the stooping and lifting."

While she dreamed on, *I* gagged with guilt over all I had been taking for granted.

A chorus of yells went up as a truck swirled into the yard in a cloud of dust and Adam and Bill hurried out to stand by as the meter man hooked up the power.

"They're ready!" screamed one of the big boys from outside. "Everybody get set!"

Like sailors manning their lifeboat stations, boys and girls of all sizes whipped through the house and stationed themselves beside doorways. Then an expectant hush fell, followed by a call from upstairs, "We're all ready! Let 'er go!"

"All set!" yelled another from outside. "Here she goes!"

The power traveled the wires and the house blazed like a Christmas tree as fifty years of progress clamored into life. The sink splashed, the refrigerator hummed and began to cool. The new range turned red and hot, while Barbara hovered lovingly over the different stages of heat as she pressed buttons and turned on the timer.

"Gee!" "Golly!" "Wouldja look at that!" and "It's on!" came from doorways as kids flipped switches upstairs and down and the lights blinked under unbelieving fingers.

The magic held them briefly and then someone pressed another switch and they streamed outside in bunches to investigate and turn on the yard light. Then they raced to the barn to switch the yard light off with another switch. They checked it again and then surged back inside the house, flipping switches madly, shouting, dancing, and racing around with the glee of a Christmas morning and a package so huge its unwrapping goes on and on.

Bill told me later Adam had led him to the barn and the electric milking machine, and on to the shop to try the electric drill. He drilled boards that didn't need holes, as he dreamed of future electric sanders and saws, of fences for his cattle.

"This is going to be a great winter!" he beamed. "Just wait until it freezes and I can use my car warmer! Come on to the house. Let me show you my electric razor."

As they returned to the humming, buzzing, splashing household, the oldest boy pulled at Adam's sleeve. "C'mere, Pa. I wanna show you somethin'." He led him outside and pointed to the meter now whizzing in rapid circles.

"My god! Look at all that money going up in smoke!" bellowed Adam. "Turn off those lights! Turn off that pump! *Slow down, will ya?*"

No one but Bill and I heard him. We looked at each other and laughed. The others were too excited to hear. In the living room the new vacuum cleaner was whirring though there was, as yet, no rug. Florence, the oldest daughter, ran the sewing machine and then raced over to the fancy old treadle and pushed it into a corner. In the bathroom upstairs a toilet flushed and kids' eyes danced at the splattering.

"Just think!" Florence said dreamily, "no more coal or wood to carry for the stove. No more dirt on our hands when we're cooking. No more going out to the cellar every time we need something cold for supper. Now we won't have to cook and can and smoke meat all on the same day for fear it'll spoil!"

"And all the hot water we want," Barbara added. "Now we can even take *big* baths!" But one of the kids had thought of that first and the bathtub already sloshed merrily.

And briefly. For Adam was making himself heard at last over the din. Barbara had just turned on the electric mixer and was standing, entranced, listening to its hum as he came in and ordered everything "off!" Still, the excitement and thrill of the day lingered, briefly renewing itself at dark and again later when the lights went on in bedrooms.

Bill and I retired to a brightly lighted bedroom. "Wow!" he exclaimed. "What a day! I thought sure their fuses would blow."

I nodded. "Listen. Those kids are still buzzing." We chuckled at excited whispers from the other side of the wall.

But sleep didn't come easily for me that night either. Not until I'd promised myself that fatigue and self-pity were never again going to erase the magic from reality. I blinked mist from my eyes and was warmed by an elusive feeling—as if I had been touched by the wing of a miracle. And I guess I had. Rarely is a woman given such a revealing glimpse of her own life through the unclouded eyes of children.

It was the beginning, actually, the turning point. I had had an objective look at the self-pitying drudge I had become and I couldn't stand myself. Not liking yourself is the deepest loneliness there is, and you have to regain your self-respect before you can move onward. Besides, I had to get myself together if I wanted the kids to come through early life unscathed by my own acid.

I couldn't go out to work for a change of pace and a lift to my morale. We had a business and I was chained to it. You thought only kids chained you down? A motel has them beat into the ground for binding you to home plate.

Since it was self at fault and self that needed boosting, I decided (not without some assist by our pastor) to do what I'd been advised to do years earlier when my nerves had been shot.

"Do something every day just for yourself alone," he said. "Do something *you* want to do. Pay no attention to what anyone else says or thinks. You're getting to know yourself better."

I decided to dabble again in oil paints. It had been years! They were inexpensive, I'm a nut over colors, they could be dropped at a ring of the doorbell. And it was a beginning.

Many of those earlier pictures were like any Sunday painter's—a disaster in composition, but they did what they were supposed to do. They made me feel useful and important even when no one was around to comment on them, which was usually the case.

I decided to take a course in commercial art. It was a three-year course, and Bill was as enthusiastic as I, for he'd already seen how much better I was feeling about myself in this lift-yourself-by-your-paintbrush project.

I finished two years of the course and I knew I'd hit another milestone when I realized the course was taking a tack I didn't like. When I got into calligraphy and was expected to print letters and words all over my pictures, I called a halt. By now I'd become confident enough to make a decision that didn't conform to my parents' all-time expectancy of me: "Always finish what you begin."

Why go on with something that was a pain? I chucked it and started a new hobby, creative writing. This, too, was inexpensive and could be dropped at a moment's distraction and creativity now loomed high as my greatest need. With small children underfoot and a business where scut work was multiplied even over any *large* family's expectance of the mother, creativity was my badly needed escape valve.

But here, as with painting, I found that one cannot be creative without thinking things through. Again I was turned in upon myself, but this time with a goal ahead, and I realized that what had been missing from my life for a long, long time was the nearness of God and the reliance of his wisdom to get me through my days. *Again* I was relearning how also to be a Mary.

11
Prejudice Is Emotion—
Love Is Action

Every woman needs constantly to reassess her relationship to God, for in so doing she is reevaluating, as well, her own truth and loyalty to her deepest self. It's somewhat within a woman's nature that she be constantly aware of herself. Her menstrual cycles, the world's reaction to her attractiveness or lack of it, whether or not society approves or disapproves of her expected emotionalism or its lack, which too often is taken as unattractive masculinity—all of these make us intensely aware of ourselves as persons. Unfortunately, it can also cause us to overreact by doing all we can to gain society's approval. It's inherent in all human beings to need the approval of their peers. Perhaps that's why it's so difficult sometimes to defy our own social group's conventions.

Women often bewail this need to concentrate on self and it can produce the self-absorption that easily leads to selfishness. But it doesn't have to. I prefer to think that these inherent needs for the busy Martha to be constantly concerned about herself represent rather an inborn precaution leading to her other self—the Mary. A tool given us by our Lord that helps us the more often to return to him. To reorganize the steps that endanger us by leading us into unsafe waters. He made us to be mothers, after all, and such deliberate steps of caution in helping to warn us while there is yet time to change also preserve, for our children, mothers capable of the kind of love and service to God that is so irresistible and contagious that our youngsters catch it and hold it for a lifetime.

As vital to our children as discipline is, love of God and all humankind is far greater. *But such love cannot be taught. It must be caught.* And only a mother with a Mary-Martha balance will totally succeed.

Prejudice toward difference of race, creed, or cultural origin point up as accurately as a barometer how well we are succeeding or failing. Do *you* ever nod over a bigoted act by someone else and say, "It's too bad. I'm sure glad *I'm* not prejudiced!"

Besides those words sounding disturbingly like the words of the self-righteous Pharisees whom Jesus called whited sepulchers, it simply is not true. If you're a woman, I'll bet my favorite banana nut cake recipe that in *any* argument, from party hat to politics, you assert yourself with a peculiarly prejudiced, *feminine* viewpoint.

There's nothing new about the differences between men and women. Personally, I think they make life interesting. But today women nettle excessively easily on the subject. We're just realizing what being a member of a minority group means in terms of jobs and putdowns.

Only—differences don't *have* to be all bad. But we are bogged down by actions and reactions, emotions built upon centuries of ignorance and insults until every one of us is caught in some way by the snare called prejudice.

Yet somehow we must take off our goggles and see reality so that we don't perpetuate our prejudices in our youngsters. It's such a remaking of ourselves that we couldn't do it without the beautiful example Jesus gave us of even the Samaritan's value. The biggest obstacle to remaking ourselves is that we too often fail to realize we need it.

A woman I know, a real estate broker, denies vehemently

having any prejudice toward a living soul. Yet the first time she was in our house she looked at the oil painting of the Sacred Heart of Jesus that hung on the living room wall and said, "Oh. You're Catholics. I am too. I know it shouldn't make any difference," she smiled knowingly, "but somehow it does."

No one is completely unprejudiced toward those of other status, other faiths, other national descents, *or* toward those with different skin color.

What is prejudice, exactly? Much of the racial furor raging today is due to a misconception of the word. Webster defines it as "to prepossess with unexamined opinion, or opinions formed without due knowledge of the facts and circumstances attending the question; to bias judgment of, by hasty and incorrect notions and give it an unreasonable bent to one side or other of a cause."

In other words, *prejudice is incorrect.* It's an *emotion* preceding the knowledge which could balance the judgment and foster understanding and Christian love.

Have you ever noticed how a person's appearance changes after you've known him for a time? When I was a small girl, my father brought home to dinner a tall, spare man who was extremely ugly. His face bore heavy lines that made me want to duck and run. I had to be scolded and forcibly seated at the table across from him. But before dinner was over, I began to notice how much he smiled. Those deep lines were rings and rings of laugh wrinkles put there by years of being the kindest and finest of men.

He visited us often after that, and after the first shock of meeting him, his face grew in pleasing appearance in direct proportion to our friendship. When I knew the real man, I no longer saw the difference between us.

Some of the most fervent denials of bigotry come from minority groups suffering from its consequences themselves, yet who can't see the beam in their own eyes.

I know I cannot deny my prejudices, because by prejudice

I do *not* mean actions toward others, which can be hate or love or somewhere in between. I'm referring to that inner emotion that wells up inside when you meet or talk with anyone different from yourself.

As Christian mothers, we owe our children a balanced view of this world. As Mary-Martha mothers, we should be showing them that in real Christianity, often the actions showing love must come *before* the emotion. We do this best by showing them how *we* make the first, the compassionate move toward a fellow human being who is different.

Keeping the women's liberation discussion out of our dinner dialogue is one way. It's a valid issue, yes, but the kids needn't get a closeup of it, especially if it's critical of the dad they love. We are obliged by our very membership in the Mystical Body of Christ, to love all humankind in his name. To treat any and all human beings with the real charity (love) which St. Paul described:

> If I speak in the tongues of men and of angels, but have not love, I am a noisy gong or a clanging cymbal. And if I have prophetic powers, and understand all mysteries and all knowledge, and if I have all faith, so as to remove mountains, but have not love, I am nothing. If I give away all I have, and if I deliver my body to be burned, but have not love, I gain nothing.
>
> Love is patient and kind; love is not jealous or boastful; it is not arrogant or rude. Love does not insist on its own way; it is not irritable or resentful; it does not rejoice at wrong, but rejoices in the right. Love bears all things, believes all things, hopes all things, endures all things. . . . So faith, hope, love abide, these three; but the greatest of these is love [I Corinthians 13:1-7;13].

We may succeed only in making a beginning. We may be generations ridding ourselves of bigoted attitudes that have sprung from faulty environment and its background. But we must put forth that first step, *act* like the Christians we ought to be, so that our children will some day *feel* that way.

Before I joined the Catholic Church, I often heard anti-

Catholic jibes about the "fisheaters." It's unfortunate but true that in the thirty-seven years I've been a Catholic, I've heard as many anti-Protestant remarks from Catholics. I've never heard bigotry preached from the pulpit in our church; but there are still laymen who find quiet but deadly effective means to cut down people who are different and to cut them off.

It's easy to fall into the habit of noncommunication with anyone different from ourselves. That, it seems to me, is the crux of the whole problem. How, then, can we learn about non-Catholics, Jews, blacks, Chicanos, (whatever we are *not*)—and grow in understanding and love for them?

Why should not non-Catholics believe what they've heard about Catholics? That we are shepherded, unthinking masses. That we suffer our faith in silence (that'll be the day!)? So *many* of us shy away from any discussion of religion as if we were involved in a clandestine affair, instead of the affairs of the mystical Body of Christ itself.

Once I was extremely prejudiced against Catholics. Now I've moved to the other side with, I hope, a little more understanding. Unfortunately, I find I'm still a little prejudiced *if we speak only of emotion.* Yet to be true to Christ and to myself as a mother striving toward the Mary-Martha ideal, I must restrain unpleasant emotions, rash judgments toward others *and* their faiths. *None of these, no matter how deeply felt, must be permitted to color the way I act or write or speak.* For the way I act invariably will in turn color the way my children will act.

I'm sorry to have to say that occasionally emotions *do* promote some rash action I'm later sorry for. Perhaps it's my own weakness that makes me say that bigotry, the racial tug of war, won't be stopped within a few short years. We may conquer actions. We will not so easily harness emotions. Nor, once harnessed, will emotions easily vanish.

My background is not one to have built undue prejudice

toward blacks. I was born in the state of Washington and lived there and in California where there are many blacks. Six of my teen years were spent on the tiny island of Aruba, Netherlands West Indies, where the native village was policed by blacks. Ouc family felt very close to Alice, our black maid. Yet today it seems odd to me that we felt no incongruity, no compunction at all, in knowing the natives had to pay for drinking water that had to be shipped in, water we received free. Yet we really believed in human rights and all the other platitudes that don't mean a thing until they are exercised.

On one of our trips to Aruba, the oil tanker on which we were passengers was dispatched up the Orinoco River in Venezuela before going on to Aruba. There we met racial bigotry in reverse. Though we had never consciously mistreated nor even ignored blacks, the dark-skinned customs official glowered at us and snarled, "I've been to your country. I went to college there. And because of my black skin I was treated like dirt. Well, now you're in *my* country, and you'll get no better here."

We were hurt, as he no doubt had been, and puzzled. The whole incident sounds like something out of the deep south today. Prejudice every day is still backing up statements by a different kind of prejudice. One group thinks that because they want what's right and good, they automatically are always right. While the other group believes they are right for the same ridiculous reason.

What has happened to charity and understanding? Worse. What are these emotional adults doing to their children? Must our worst sides always be perpetuated?

A white woman doesn't have to feel all warm and glowing inside at, say, having a black nurse in a hospital. Why not merely hold back judgment as you would with anyone else? Is there any reason a skin color should make you act un-Christian? Everyone needs outgoing love and consideration, and our offering them immediately brands us as bearing witness to Christ. There *may* follow, if the nurse is a good and helpful one, the friendship that would come in any case. But it simply cannot be there while she is strange and different and we shouldn't expect it to be.

During the Second World War, I worked in a shipyard as an electrician-welder beside another woman welder, Birdie, a black who was a college graduate and who for years had been the principal of a high school in Texas. When I first met her, I was very aware of that strangeness, that "difference" which I feel for anyone who is different from myself—and that is everyone I've ever met.

It was almost a week before Birdie and I made the mutual discovery that we both liked egg salad sandwiches and dill pickles. Only then began the feminine chitchat which knows no color line. We lunched and reminisced about our homes and tried to explain away the peculiar problems each of us had because of the different colors of our skins.

Though as a black she had received more insults than I had at the time, I had tasted of insults and prejudice, too, when I joined the Catholic Church against the wishes of family and friends. And religious jibes begun at my baptism were many years dissipating.

I don't necessarily like black skin. But then neither do I like my own freckled skin. I much prefer that ethereal petal-pink-and-white skin that I don't believe I've ever seen. So what?

We don't live in a dream world. We live in a world of Protestants, Catholics, and Jews; professional men and laborers; dark-skinned and white. Our lives are full of differences. Some day, God willing, we will all learn to accept each other with something akin to our acceptance and tolerance today of those strangest of all creatures, the opposite sex.

My own bigotry is a bit more squelched every time I, as a Catholic, remember a song I used to sing as a Protestant child in Sunday School. "Red and yellow, black and white; they are precious in his sight. Jesus loves the little children of the world."

But we cannot completely squelch our own bigotry, just as we cannot accomplish *any* spiritual growth on our own. The good God is waiting to show us the way, to help us to grow, and he's as near as our hearts. See what he says: "O Jerusalem, Jerusalem, killing the prophets and stoning those who are sent to you! How often would I have gathered your children together as a hen gathers her brood under her wings, and you would not! Behold, your house is forsaken and desolate. For I tell you, you will not see me again, until you say, 'Blessed is he who comes in the name of the Lord' " (Matthew 23:37–39). What, then, are we waiting for? When we speak to glorify him, he hears our every word.

This is the simple lesson which has such far-reaching results. The lesson we must first teach our own tangled emotions. Then through simple association—as all teaching is— our young people will accept others with the openness and love they knew before the outside world and their own families distorted it.

Seeds of prejudice are within every one of us, in one way or another; and they are the Christian problem of the dignity of all humankind and this makes them first in importance to the family. Through our Lord, you and I are called as Christians and as Mary-Martha mothers to work woman to child, woman to woman, and family to family for ever-increasing growth in love, each for the other. As St. Paul said so well: "There is one body and one Spirit, just as you were called to the one hope that belongs to your call, one Lord, one faith, one baptism, one God and Father of us all, who is above all and through all and in all" (Ephesians 4:4–6).

12
Everyone Counts
in a Family Council

The ideal of the Christian home, of course, is the Holy Family. Yet probably every mortal mother, at one time or another, has breathed desperately, as I have, "Sure, but Jesus was a *perfect* Child! I wonder what Mary and Joseph would have done with Larry. Or Tom. Or Bobbi. Or *any* of ours."

Ours is a family where only a scant sampling of daily happenings are: a son who takes two and a half hours "dressing" in the morning. A daughter who one day cut up her pajamas in a rage of jealousy over a new baby. A miniature David who turned a loaded squirt gun on a mighty older brother capable of tearing him apart—who might have, had I not intervened. A sincere second grade show-and-teller who found a sister's secret cache of love poems and sowed them broadcast over the school.

Did the Boy Jesus ever harass his mother in ways like these? I can't believe it.

Having faith in God and praying often and fervently (oh yes!) is vital, for there are gaps in our lives we cannot fill by ourselves. A Martha could never bail herself out of the predicaments our kids have put me into. Recognizing a Mary side, while a comfort, is not quite a total answer either. For from the above motley crew I *still* had to fashion human beings of love and responsibility and no mortal woman can do such an immortal job without help that's out of this world.

I think it was the Holy Spirit who answered my pleas by sending me the idea of the family council. Now a family council may not answer all the ills that beset a family on its rocky road to Christian maturity, but Bill and I think it comes pretty close.

True to my Martha nature, I didn't even realize Darryl, then a tow-headed five-year-old, was having problems until his kindergarten teacher sent home a note saying he was not cooperating. I tried to shrug this off as one of the many constant and not too great crises that happen in a family which then contained eleven youngsters.

After her note, however, I noticed that Darryl was silent most of the time and that blonde little Bobbi, eight, and Lolly, four, had somehow become lost, too, in the rising tide of busyness and words and needs that swirled over and around them. Darryl ate his meals in total silence. The only time he relaxed was around the children at play. At the table or wherever he had to compete with others for attention from Bill or me, he seemed to have given up. He just sat with giant accusing eyes, while Bobbi or Lolly meekly followed along with the other girls or sat alone.

Guilt was my first reaction. Next came a semblance of common sense and the sensitivity to others that helped me grow into a Mary too. Finally the action. I had read somewhere that family councils were a fine place to air teenage feelings and we had three teen-agers, also, who were loaded with gripes. Fine, I thought, we'll fix those too.

We held our first council after the Sunday midday dinner, since all but I were dragging their feet and there simply was no other time coercion might work.

"Do we need a book on *Robert's Rules of Order?*" asked our junior high student. "If you do, I've got one from school."

"Go get it then, Bonnie, please. We need something." And I noted with satisfaction that she was one teen-ager who already felt so important her gripes had temporarily vanished.

When I insisted, the children loudly scuffled their way back to the table, the three older boys with snorts, whistles, and shoves; the girls with groans and dramatics; the babies with thumbs and smiles. I looked down the eighty-four-inch formica-topped table lined with squirming, nudging humanity and wondered if even *Robert's Rules of Order* could produce quiet and efficiency out of these noisy samples of humanity.

From chaos and clamoring we finally brought the commotion down to a low hum. Madame Chairman turned out to be me. Bill turned down the honor on grounds that this did not sound like a very good way to get his Sunday rest. I accepted the position only with the understanding that each of the three older twelve would take turns being chairman.

"—and each one of us gets to say what we think? Even about things we *don't* like?" asked Peggy in wide-eyed disbelief.

"Especially about what you don't like."

Larry's round, sun-tanned face was shocked, his mouth open. Finally he said, *"Every single one of us?"* He jerked a thumb at Vickie, still in the high chair chortling happily.

"If you want to say anything, yes." And I noticed Lolly was still silent, tugging on a lock of red-brown hair, her hazel eyes downcast.

"Then I make a motion we have new bedtimes!" Larry, who was twelve, declared triumphantly. "Separate bedtimes should be set for each kid. Everybody over ten shouldn't have to go to bed with the babies!"

My husband shot me a glance that said clearly, "See? It's going to blow up in our faces."

But it was at this point we rediscovered the wonderful

capacity children have for being just—as long as they understand the reasoning involved.

"Let's have some discussion before we take a vote," I hedged. "I want each one of you to think about whether you really need a new bedtime. Is it wise to stay up after you're tired and sleepy? If you do decide you want the time changed and bedtimes become scattered all over the clock, how will any of us remember who goes to bed when? We aren't super-parents, you know."

"You know it!" exclaimed Janice, and the circle of faces around the table grinned, giggled, and nodded. "But all of us who can tell time can remember our own times. We won't fudge."

"Madame Chairman?" Bill said, "I think we've just hit a big snag that's going to push this whole project under, unless you and I load the odds."

The moans and groans around the table were as acute as if he had removed a turkey drumstick from the mouth of each.

"I thought it was too good to be true!" exploded Larry.

"Wait a minute, kids! Dad's got a point and since we've all agreed to listen to each other, why don't you listen to Dad too?"

Most of them hung their heads and looked shamefaced. "OK," Larry said grudgingly, "I suppose I can listen."

"What I was trying to say," Bill explained, "is there are some matters important to the kids' health and the state of affairs around here. After all, we're responsible for their lives and we have to be allowed to carry the vote on these points."

"Is our bedtime one of those points?" Larry asked with the directness of a district attorney.

Bill looked at me and flushed a little. Obviously he didn't want to put a crimp in all this fine democracy. Just as obviously, he had dumped the role of dirty dog onto me.

"I'd say it might be," I quibbled, "but, like most things, it wouldn't have to be, as long as the family uses good judgment."

Bill's suggestion, with juvenile embellishments, became a motion and reluctantly it was seconded and passed. What happened next would have jolted a stranger as much as it did Bill and me. For each child had a stake in this problem and though Darryl and Lolly remained silent, Bobbi's blonde hair tossed as her blue eyes sparked into interest.

"I think we ought to go to bed early on school nights. But we should get to stay up late and watch TV on Fridays and Saturday nights," came from this unbelievable eight-year-old mouth.

A mature discussion then began to flow forth, one at a time for a refreshing change, until even Lolly's eyes lifted and she spoke up, "Me too."

"But go to bed early Sunday night because Monday's a school day and we have to get up early," ended Larry. All heads bobbed and there were three seconds. I stole an I-told-you-so look at Bill.

When I asked all in favor to raise their hands, all hands lifted but Darryl's. Still soberly unblinking, he only looked on.

"All those against the motion that we change bedtimes raise their hands," I said to him.

Still he did not respond.

"Darryl, you didn't vote. We have to know which way you want it, before we know what to do about the family's bedtimes."

He sat there for another moment, just gaping. Then he swallowed painfully and whispered in awe, "Y'—mean— *I* get to say *too?*"

"Yes. You're every bit as important to this family as any one of us. We want to know what you think too."

"You mean—*me too?*" The incredulity in his voice was heartbreaking. How had we ever let him grow so far away from us?

"Yeah, ya creep, step on it!" Larry prodded in the way of brothers. "Vote, will ya? We don't want to be here all day!"

"Come on, runt," Brian added affectionately.

"Boys!"

"Well, gee—I—." The blue eyes finally blinked and took on a new gleam and his shoulders pulled up. He shifted in his seat and finally words began to tumble out. "Well, I want to go to bed when I get tired, too, instead of just 'cause!"

Everybody sighed and relaxed, but none more than I.

Bonnie raised her hand and when I nodded, said, "I move we all choose our own jobs, too, instead of being told what to do." And into this problem all waded with assurance, even Darryl. He was the first to raise his hand. At this Bill flashed me worry signals as if he feared our family had cast loose all ties and was heading for the precipice. But the others were no longer anxious over what either parent thought.

"I'd rather vacuum the rug than carry out the garbage," Darryl said firmly.

"And I'd rather do the dishes again than to have a job that takes all day and all night," Tom added.

"Me too. I want to take out the garbage. It stinks, but it isn't hard." Bobbi beamed proudly when no one disagreed.

Thus the jobs were reapportioned by popular vote and individual choice and I had even obtained a new dishwasher who smiled over the job.

Our five-year-old, however, had found a new and giddy world. His arm immediately shot up again. When acknowledged, he said, "Can I say if something's no good?"

"Yes. That's what the meeting is for."

He took a big wavery breath and blurted, as if it were one word, "Well-I-think-nobody-should-get-spanked-for-not-doing-little-things-like-spilling-his-milk-and-not-feeding-his-dog." After it was out, he leaned back and he was trembling!

"Nobody wants to spank a boy for a little thing, Darryl," I said over a painful lump in my throat. "And to get spanked for spilling your milk is wrong and I'm glad you brought it up. Dad and I'll try not to get too angry again, so we can remember."

His blue eyes blazed in warmth and glory.

Bonnie's hand was in the air this time and when I nodded, she said, "But not feeding the dog is not a *little* thing! It's a big thing. What if poor Lady had somebody feeding her who always forgot? Why, she'd die!"

"What do the rest of you think?"

The others noisily proclaimed judgment against Darryl and finally even he agreed, with a very tiny nod of his head and a puzzled but very satisfied little smile on his face.

Experienced parents, especially those who have tried family councils, know that meetings which attempt to bind together all ages of people almost never are as smooth as they sound. Our first hurdle, where Bill and I loaded the odds in extreme cases, had been safely passed.

But before all of the children learned how to conduct themselves at a business meeting and were totally willing to do so, there were a couple of minor skirmishes. I settled these by telling them this was like any other game. If they didn't want to abide by the rules, they could leave the table and go to their rooms until they wanted to cooperate. At the word *cooperate* I smiled fondly over at Darryl, who this time returned it with a look of such dazzling love that tears jumped to my eyes.

What happened to him the following week in school I only learned at the next PTA meeting, when his teacher grabbed me by the arm and almost spilled my coffee.

"Oh—I'm sorry, Mrs. Hertz! But I'm so glad to see you. I've been wanting to talk to you about Darryl." Oh no! I groaned inwardly. What was wrong now? "I don't know what's happened to that boy, but the change is absolutely miraculous! Did you tell him to cooperate better with the children? If you did, he certainly seems to have gone all out. And he looks so much happier!"

I explained the workings of our family council.

"You mean you let even *kindergartners* have a voice in running the family?" she exclaimed in amazement and considerable disapproval. Then she brightened again. "But he has changed—I thought sure you'd told him to get along better with the others."

I didn't say so, but "telling" a child to get along is about my last resort, if I really want him to join in with others. But I had noticed Darryl's change of attitude in other areas too. This boy, who had been silent and so little trouble we had forgotten him, who had desperately needed the approval of someone who cared, had suddenly discovered that not one or two but the entire family did care very much what he said and did. He began to speak up to Bill and me. Most encouraging of all, he began teasing Lolly. When the mischief began, I knew he had returned to normal.

Love is strange. It really doesn't matter whether you love someone, he can't feel that love until you manage, somehow, to communicate your feelings to him. I had become so engrossed and distracted I had momentarily neglected the individual attention Darryl and all children deserve and require. I was even more shaken to realize that children could so completely believe they were unloved even when their parents loved them dearly. That I had not listened, really listened, when our kids were right there showing by their silence and behavior what they felt or feared.

Our family is no more ideal than any other. But then I don't really know what an ideal family is. All of those I've known make their mistakes. And one of the biggest mistakes we mothers make is allowing other things to infringe on our minds until we only *half* listen—which most youngsters take as more insulting than turning our backs on them entirely.

Our children are of the first generation born with the Bomb in their cribs, and with threat of nuclear holocaust held before them daily by mass communications media. That their nervous systems survive at all is a miracle. The heavy, constant dread that is a basic ingredient of today's youthful personalities and their future is something they desperately need to unload onto someone who cares—their parents. Especially since this heavy, constant dread is one we parents have never known. It *has* to be, therefore, a major and almost universal cause of the communication crevasse.

If children are loved and they feel it and know it, they can weather almost any condition, even the threat of global war. The children of London in World War II showed that. Because of grave dangers during the blitz, they were removed to safety. But during the trial period, they suffered more from insecurity and fright away from their parents than they had in London with blockbusters dropping all around them.

Our children have amply proven that love does *not* spring into being just because mom and dad love each other and their family. Nor does it "just happen" as they grow up, if we are good responsible mothers who try to mind our p's and q's. Because there's all of a to z looming up and snatching from our youngsters the family values we've been sowing. If we don't cement family values and love for them very, very early, our way-out society will take its inevitable toll.

Family time and sharing of experiences grow increasingly precious as we see a modern world relentlessly remove from the family circle one area of training after another—in some families leaving emotional ruin in its wake.

The closeness fostered in family councils, I think, could have prevented some of today's crop of alcoholics and other drug addicts, young people who can't stand themselves and who find copping out the only bearable way to cower before a painful and unendurable future.

Such dread *must* be unloaded, weakened by sharing it. Young people need to sound out their parents. They need to see exactly why you and I are not running off and committing suicide or why we don't blank out on liquor or drugs.

If we have never listened, how will we know when the time has come to explain that one sleeping pill is used, not as escape, but often as a road to better productivity? That one or two drinks is not like getting habitually smashed to shut out the world because we can't face up to it? *That moderation is the key to keeping command of a situation and of a life and even of a society?*

Where did I get all this philosophy? They are direct quotes from our long series of family councils that after some time disintegrated into family "talks" which are now family "rap" sessions. But it was the family council that first produced the kind of give-and-take discussion where the child feels no threat of being cut off or closed out or punished. And the mother (and father) is presented with ideas so shocking her attention is guaranteed to weld her to her seat and to the needs of her children. More—a circle of love is set up whereby the child gains the same kind of close group acceptance some can't find at home, so they seek it in a pot party or a kegger. Or from one of the better controlled sensitivity-training sessions geared to better communications.

In the family council, I think the finest kind of interpersonal relationships can be built and safely guided, so that unfolding personalities can securely face the uncertain world.

Now our thirteen children are old enough that we can view, through the accuracy of hindsight, the positive values of the family council. How floods of words, so seldom effective alone as communication, were directed into a real rapport. Child guidance mistakes happen in all families, large and small, and a family council may not always work miracles, but we don't know of another system that can produce the same harmony as ours has.

Darryl is now twenty-three and a year out of college; both he and our two college students, as well as the two in high school, often bring into our family, for open discussion, their worries and concerns over the alcohol and other drug availability, the sex revolution, the sins of the Establishment.

It is not uncommon for one to come home with another youth in tow and say, "He's got a problem, Mom. Can we talk to you?" And sometime during the ensuing chat, I usually learn that here is another one whose mother and father act as if he doesn't exist.

Bonnie, now adult, wrote a letter one day saying, "Mom and Dad, I've asked a friend of mine to stop by and talk to you for awhile. He's pretty mixed up and I know you'll be nice to him. He says he hasn't any friends. He's an alcoholic. Try to help him if you can."

We "helped" him—by listening. *Just* by listening and *not condemning.* It's really not so hard, once one learns to let everything else wait when human beings are involved.

Two of our youngsters are still at home and sometimes we'd like to overreact, when alcohol and drug abuse or other social dangers are mentioned in such a way that we know our young fledglings are feeling along their individual ways. But we have learned that confidence in young people and their ability to handle these situations pays off. It will be the day one of them closes us out that I'll feel we've slipped again.

Bill and I have discussed that possibility. We've decided that even if we feel panicky, we'll keep our cool and try to remember that trust, and the kind of communication where the mother (or father) really *listens,* can help a child weather anything. This is the proof of the love for God in the brotherhood of man (and small children) which the Mary-Martha mother holds as a continuous goal. Sensitivity formed from Christian love.

Robert Henri said it for us: "Feel the dignity of the child. Do not feel superior to him, for you are not."

13
The Holiness of Christmas

Teaching a child the holiness of Christmas is like teaching a flower to look at the sun. Trying to do either sharply points up our own shortcomings in the business of faith and love. We have to reach into the deepest recesses of ourselves to the innocence *we* first knew, to see why we are floundering today, as women, as mothers. Only as we pray for guidance and correct our own thinking can we see how very easily and unknowingly we have let these children stray from their original innocence.

It's a unique privilege that all mothers share, this sacred trust we have of showing our children the holiness of Jesus. And the logical beginning is, naturally, to first show them the holiness of Christmas. A Mary-Martha mother is one who has already become so established in her Christian beliefs that she *can* clearly let her own faith do the teaching for her.

Unfortunately, this is where I first understood how totally the world had absorbed me, and with me our children. As in so many other things, I took the long winding trail to the truth. And, as children always will, they saw through to the real me and copied *that*, not the lesson I was trying to teach them.

Like most Christian mothers, each Christmas since Tom,

our eldest, was two, I have enjoyed the long intimate hours I've shared with our children as I've told them again and again the lovely story of how Jesus was born. But have you ever wondered what the playback might be on *any* lovely story you've told your kids? I found it very disconcerting when I learned that my idea of something deep and meaningful had been turned into mishmash by the little minds that had *not* absorbed my words, but had fully assimilated my unsaid attitudes and reflected these back to me instead.

My first jolt came on a day long ago when a guest in our home asked Tom, then five, "Tommy, what do you think Christmas is, *really*?"

While I proudly waited for the beautiful holy story to pour forth, Tom grinned around a wet piece of ribbon candy and came up with, "Christmas is when we get all our stuff."

I still blush to think of it. But God gives mothers more than one chance. It seems to me we mothers do far too much sounding off about what is important to *us* under the blithe assumption that what we say is actually being learned. It appears to be an almost universal failing of parents that we believe our sermons are absorbed without question. How I wish it were so!

You may be sure Bill and I renewed our efforts to upgrade the holiness of Christmas to our children. I tried by more stories, more explanations, as well as I knew how. Yet a few years and four kids later, Larry, then six and old enough to know what it was all about, I thought, was asked a similar question.

He beamed, pushed the brown hair out of his gray eyes and looked important, as all six-year-olds in big families do when they have all attention focused upon them. Then he answered eagerly, "Christmas is when we get our Christmas tree up and fin'lly decorated and then Sandy Claus brings us our presents and everybody's happy!"

Well, I thought grimly, *If everybody's happy, I suppose that's some kind of improvement, but what's happened to Baby Jesus around here?*

My soul-searching began. Sacred Scripture tells us we shall not enter the kingdom of God unless we accept it with the approach of a child. But to set our children's hearts on a path so they may even *have* an approach is no small thing. Children have to be shown, not told, before they can bring to any story their own clear and forthright perspective. Obviously I'd not been getting through.

The older children seemed to have it all straight, but it still distressed me that the little ones did not, for I believe the earlier religious teachings reach our children, the more powerful and continuing they will be. I knew, too, that an angry child at any age hears only the deeply disturbing noise of loud voices—and doesn't even catch the words for very fear. We'd been through all that with our kids, too.

During the Christmas season maybe it was their own excitement getting in the way. And then maybe it wasn't. More likely, my own deeply weary tones of voice as a materialistic Martha, or the strain of financial burdens that weighed on Bill, had overlain our words until the beauty and holiness both of us really felt for Christmas had failed to show. A disastrous result and I knew it, yet in our big family I prepared for Christmas, even more than for other holidays, at a dead run. I had a business to look after *and* I *did* care that the children understood the depth of meaning in Christmas.

Maybe I cared too much. Often when we work outside of our homes, there is a built-in guilt and because of that we overreact and it colors our feelings and actions. Maybe my very desperation flawed the youngsters' interpretation of it. Certainly, though, they had seen the Martha that lurked beneath the surface all the while. I had emulated, but really had not yet learned to be a Mary. For a Mary would have let small details slide for this one vital point. I had tried very hard to concentrate on the beauty and holiness of Christmas.

Whatever, I had to try again. And this time I added plenty of prayer, beginning with Advent. Again I beseeched the Holy Spirit to fill in the gaps, to give me the words. Again I discussed with the children the well-loved Christmas story and I even slowed up this time, in an effort to show how vitally important the day still is for every Christian. But I was still falling short, I knew by the youngsters' feedback.

Then one beautiful Christmas Eve, Peggy, five, was the first zipped into her yellow sleepers and ready for bed. Christmas Eve—and all through the house *nobody* was quiet. Other children were still pulling on jammies and sleepers and taking noisy baths. Bill and I momentarily sagged into chairs between the crèche and the tree which was, for our family, decorated.

Did you know tinsel makes a decorative addition to the edge of a peanut butter sandwich? An effect equaled only when splendor of tinsel has met energy of child and here and there the tree's glitter is dulled by bitlets of jam and tasted candy cane, festooned with pocket fuzz and peanut butter. Even our treetop angel passes through many hands. Now she teetered atop her almost needle-bare perch, her wispy hair tangled.

"Well, Bill," I said, "they've caught the enjoyment of the Christmas *tree*, anyway, but that was a pagan symbol before the Christians adapted it. But *what is it going to take to reach those kids*? What do they really *know* about Jesus?"

Just then Peggy, sleep-sweet and rosy-cheeked, swept to the floor with a flourish beside my chair, made a wide and equally impressive Sign of the Cross, and eagerly began to say her prayers. At our house this has always been a private time. The one moment in the day when each child, in turn, could claim God's and my undivided attention. The soft words tumbling from her lips in the accent she still retained from babyhood began to answer my frustrated question. Her fair hair clung damply to her neck, where tiny tendrils snuggled close.

After the prayers her gray eyes looked into mine and she seemed about to burst. "Muvver," she asked, "can I tell you the story about Baby Jesus?"

"That would be very nice," I invited.

She put one loving arm cozily around my neck so she could see that my attention wouldn't waver as it far too often did with seven other little ones to tend. But she needn't have worried, for I became caught up in the magic story with her very first words:

"One day Mawy—that's the Bwessed Muvver—sat on a donkey that has long ears and a tail that switches like the bwanch of a twee. An' she sat on the donkey *all* the way from her own house to a pwace far, far away called Beth—Beth—a big city that didn't have any motel wooms left. It was like our vacation, Muvver, on'y they didn't dwive to another city. They stopped wight there! An' St. Joseph—that's Mawy's daddy—he wooked and wooked until he found a pwace for them to sweep.

"It was a *big* cave with stwaw and stuff and lots of soft, warm, furry animals like sheeps and cows and donkeys and even a camel with a big fuzzy hump, I think. A cave is a special pwace where animals stay and it has a thing in it where cows eat fwom. An' inside the cave, Mawy—that's the Bwessed Muvver—went to a corner and wested.

"But St. Joseph, who was big and stwong like daddy, he cweaned and cweaned so they could sweep there. He even cweaned the pwace where the cows eated their hay, an' he put nice cwean stwaw there too.

"An' *then* the nice warm cows with big brown eyes and wong tails that's for shooin' fwies started to come over to wook at Baby Jesus, too, but they didn't either. Come over, I mean. They just come cwose enough to *barewy* peek at the bwand new Baby! An' there was the woolly sheeps, too, that baaed and baaed and wanted to come to see Baby Jesus, too, but they didn't either. They just stood back wike nice kids an' wooked and wooked and wooked. An' even the donkeys was so supwised at Baby Jesus *they* started to go see the teeny Baby. But they didn't either. They just stood there with their wong ears stickin' up, wistening to evewything. An' all the animals bwew out their funny-smewing bweaths in the air, an' all of 'em wooked happy.

"An' all the time Mawy—that's the Bwessed Muvver—held her baby cwose as she could and just wuved him because he was God's Baby too. An' he was borned so he could wearn us how to wuv evewybody.

"An' *then* St. Joseph took Baby Jesus in his big hairy arms that are just like daddy's, and put him in the stwaw pwace so evewybody could come and see him. An' some even bwought him pwesents 'cause it was his birfday.

"An *then* there was men called shepherds that saw a big, big star that was making it all wight outside to show 'em where Baby Jesus was. It was shinin' as *hard* as ever it could so all the people all awound would know Jesus was borned.

"An' *then* there was angels with big wings up in the sky, all gwowing an' they was singing 'Gwowy to God.' " Peggy looked around and sighed in sheer joy. And so did Bill and I, and all of the other children who had, one by one, tiptoed in to sit down and listen.

"An' 'cause evewybody bwought him pwesents, *that's* why Santy Cwaus started giving pwesents to evewybody and that's why evewybody still does. Give pwesents, I mean. 'Cause Chwistmas is Jesuses birfday." Her gray eyes had grown huge and her face was filled with wonder and something more. A certainty so beautiful tears stung my eyes and I gulped, but she had one thing more to say.

"Muvver—can I bwow out the candle on Jesuses birfday cake? *He* won't care. *He* wuvs me!"

Again, the children had learned in spite of, not because of, me. Through my prayers and efforts and in spite of my failings, somehow innocence had returned to innocence. And I was the one who learned the lesson in one more step toward the Mary-Martha balance.

14
God and the
Nervous Mother

God knows *no one* needs the balance of both the Mary and the Martha as much as the overemotional mother, for she is always an extreme of one or the other or a wavering between the two. When an emotional trauma reduced me to an irritable witch, it seemed more a trap than the step forward it actually was. I swung from overzeal for housework to self-absorption, with panic clutching at me each time the pendulum of emotionalism moved again. I didn't know then, as I do now, that such despair was my soul crying for help. God's loving care was with me all through that dreadful time, but I couldn't see it because my emotional state had turned me around. I saw myself only as an unthanked, unnecessary drudge who could easily be displaced by a more cheerful housekeeper.

It had all begun when we already had ten children and I became pregnant again. I hated to tell Bill, and when I finally did, I waited for him to groan. And for the eleventh time he did not.

He loves children far more than I, I thought grimly, because *I* was groaning inside. *How can he accept it just like that? Where can we put another one? How will we ever be able to pay for it?* The last baby had been a full breech and

I'd had an agonizing delivery dangerous for both him and
me. I was thirty-four. Sure, we were getting by, but barely,
though our business brought in what would have been a nice
income for a smaller family.

Bill's blue eyes warmed as tenderly as they did whenever
he picked up one of the little ones. "I wouldn't know what to
do without a baby around, anyway. They sure do grow
fast!" He cocked his head at the toddler, eleven months old
and already climbing the cupboards. "Look how big he is!
Before long he'll be in school and then where will we be?"

He didn't mention the bills, nor did he have to say he was
worried. I knew him well enough to know he was and that,
too, hurt me. The burden was always as great on him as on
me. *How will we ever get those medical bills paid if I keep on
having babies? Where is it all going to end?*

At my age I still had ten, probably fifteen, childbearing
years ahead of me! I could have another ten kids! I sat down,
suddenly weak at the very thought. Then I got up to turn
away from Bill, grateful for his quick acceptance of his
responsibility, sure, but angry with him, too, for not realizing how *jammed* I felt in our small apartment.

But my feelings must have shown on my face for Bill
pulled me around into his arms, lifted my chin up so I had to
look into his eyes, and said, "Honey, nobody ever said doing
things the way we feel God wants us to was going to be
easy."

"No," I agreed wearily, "and don't bug me with the clichés.
I know! 'For every baby God provides another loaf of
bread.' "

He chuckled. "Now *that* one has already stood the test.
Remember when I got a job the day after Tom was born and
from then on it got easier?"

"I know, Bill. Easier but more work. I know. But it doesn't
feel as if it's going to be OK this time. I'm depressed and worried."

Just then a small hand tugged at my skirt. "Mommy, can I have another samwich?" It was Darryl. I'd long ago learned that boys, for some reason, need feeding oftener than new babies. I swear they spend most of their childhood on a four-hour schedule or closer! At least ours went through the kitchen that often, and kept it wiped out of anything edible.

I sighed and went in to make him a peanut butter and jelly sandwich. And not until he was wiping jelly from his mouth with his sleeve and I jumped, salvaged the shirt, and sank into a chair again, did I have time to return to my dismal thoughts.

Somehow I got through those first days of adjustment and eventually began to search for places to take up the slack, tuck in another bed, and make another place at the table so a few months from now Mark could be put onto the bench and thus free the high chair.

But most important of all, before the end of the second month, I began to look forward. To remember that with tiny babies, especially, there is always an excellent excuse for reading while I cuddled and fed them. Maybe there *was* room in the family for another. And of course feeding was never a problem. I have always had a talent for cooking more than we could eat. With a family as large as ours, we could absorb two or three without noticing it in effort or expense. I knew how to stretch dollars and food and still keep everyone healthy. I sent a grateful prayer aloft that we had our own cow and raised our own beef, the two musts that have always been so expensive. God *had* provided most generously in the real necessities. I was prepared to have and to love our next baby.

The next thing I knew it was those crucial few days of what might have been my menstrual period two months after conception, and I began cramping and bleeding. By the time I hurried to the obstetrician, he could only confirm my fears.

"I'm sorry, Jacky, but you've already lost the baby."

We were still in the examining room and I burst into inconsolable tears. After the outburst I looked at the doctor, who was patiently waiting for me to calm down. Suddenly I felt sheepish.

"I don't know what I'm blubbering about," I blubbered. "I know it must seem silly for anyone who already has ten kids to bawl like this over a miscarriage!" And I was off again, sobbing.

He put a comforting arm around me. "No, Jacky. It's *not* silly for a woman, no matter how many kids she has, to cry over a miscarriage and to feel the loss deeply. Nature does marvelously complex things with people. Pregnant women become as emotionally prepared for childbirth as they do physically. That's why miscarriages or abortions, either, are at least as hard on the mother as a normal birth, and they're usually much harder."

I had to go home and face Bill with the unhappy news. He frowned, pulled me into his arms, rocked me, and said, "It must be what God wants. Sometimes we can't figure out what's going on, but things will work out. Don't feel too bad."

But I did. Together we said we'd just pick up the pieces of our suddenly shattered plans, but for Bill it seemed to come far more easily than for me. He was relieved in a way, I know.

Only I didn't get over it so easily. For a long time after I turned into an "overemotional" woman. And I suppose those who have never been there can't realize the real physical as well as emotional differences excessive emotion can make in the way a woman looks at her world. I would be feeling wonderful one moment, and plunge into the depths the next and over nothing more disastrous than one child tugging at another's hair. Or because Bill was half an hour late getting home. Such minute pressures totally undid me.

Of course, the family felt it almost as deeply as I, but I

wasn't thinking of them. A mother's emotions might as well be posted on the picture window, for they're always exposed nakedly to God, her family, *and* her world, if not at the moment, then when the family reacts to others.

I became as distraught and cranky as Martha the day she asked, "Lord, do you not care that my sister has left me to serve alone? Tell her to help me," (Luke 10:40). I was as overworked and nervous before the world's standards as Martha, and my Marthaisms got on everyone else's nerves too.

The "nervous mother" is a label that others not afflicted by emotionalism have glued to women such as I was during that distressing time. The relaxed person often thoughtlessly gives the label another lick. Many women have never experienced the flighty, sometimes hysterical feelings of the emotional mother—though I believe most mothers go through such feelings at one time or another in their lives. For many it's the week before the menses. Others find the months after a baby's birth especially crucial. Or, like me, the weeks or months following a miscarriage. My weeks of "nerves" gave me an inside view of the understanding and compassion needed by those whose natures have always been "overemotional" according to the world. Some call them neurotics.

It doesn't take many weeks to earn the name, and we can be crucified to that label as quickly and as surely as our children can be to one which boxes them in. Remember the rusty old saying that the difference between a psychotic and a neurotic is that one doesn't recognize reality, while the other recognizes it but just can't *stand* it?

I often wonder how the world would react today to the violent, impulsive, and highly sensitive St. Paul if he were to pay us a modern visit. *He* wasn't satisfied with the world he lived in either! And he sought to change it. Today he, too, might be labeled a neurotic.

Like the poor, God must love neurotics, for he made so

many of them. But let's forget what others say and examine who and what a neurotic mother really is.

Though all women have their nervous times which make "nerves" seem a universal female problem, many women take their emotions in stride, while others suffer a more or less perpetual neurosis, be it caused by illness, too many children, too many too fast, or a lack of innate ability to handle even one. It's those who cannot take their emotions in stride who so easily come unglued without God's help. It can also be those who, like me, try to combine business and motherhood as I did after the miscarriage as if nothing had happened—and suddenly I was on a hapless merry-go-round with no way to get off.

God, heredity, and environment have made the nervous mother what she is—different. Out of step with the world as others see it. But our highly tense society accentuates negative emotions even while condemning those who crumble most easily under pressure. The persons who commit no greater sin than to react as their Creator expects them to.

Only there is another aspect emotional women either forget or of which they are unaware—the great unhappiness they cause others. It seems as if one must be on the way to emotional stability again before she can see what she has done and is doing to her family and her friends. Whether she is a Martha who gets picky over a dust mote, or a Mary who blithely ignores the needs of her family, both are turned inward upon themselves and their needs alone—and they are equally difficult to live with.

I shall never forget the time I discovered how my ingrown attitudes were affecting our family. After work Bill walked through the door, pecked me on the cheek, then sank into a nearby chair with a "Whew! What a hell of a day! I don't think I could lift one leg after the other another minute. I've *had* it."

I whirled on him like a dervish. *"You've* had it! You've had a *glorious* day, compared to mine, holed up in this two-by-four joint with all these noisy kids. I should get a *chance* to run off and even *work* with somebody higher than my knee once!"

His blue eyes deepened with hurt and a wave of shame flooded me, but I was too tensed up, too angry, too selfish to stop and even comfort him. But I did turn and get busy with the dishes. And hours later I did apologize, but it was too late to mend the cutting blow my lack of understanding had produced.

For days thereafter I did some heavy thinking about where my explosions and unkindnesses, my sharpness with the children, were leading us all. I discovered that I couldn't increase my spiritual life or blame others—they're always so easy to blame—nor could I even blame society, with its accusing finger pointed at all neurotics, until I had carefully reviewed what was happening right here in my family.

It was the turning point. For right there lay the answer. It was the first time since the miscarriage that I had placed the family before myself, even in my thoughts.

I guess there are neurotic women who allow their nerves and self-pity to control them completely and permanently and who don't care. In every stratum of society there are irresponsible and tyrranical people; and such women do use their nerves to escape their share in life's problems while gaining undeserved sympathy as they whine and make demands, yet manage to make their families bear the guilt. In tyranny a selfish woman never had it so good, for nerves are so nebulous only they know for sure whether they can help themselves or not.

I found there is a terribly fine line between the inescapably nervous woman innocently caught in the meshes of her own instability—and the tyrannical one who takes warmth from her family and just keeps on taking without giving anything of herself in return. The latter reminds me of a prune that takes warmth from the blazing sun, not to sweeten, but to shrivel bitterly and to tighten up into itself. Like the woman, its skin—even as her conscience?—eventually becomes so hardened that no more warmth can find its way through.

Being emotionally unstable, even temporarily, can make one teeter like Humpty Dumpty between personal and often selfish needs and the needs of others. Sooner or later, though, she has to make up her mind which way she wants to fall, for she can't stay on the wall forever. The world of her loved ones, *her* world, won't stand still for it endlessly.

It's peculiar to the personality of a human being that we cannot find ourselves by ourselves alone. If we try it, we find we're on a dead-end street. Only the love of God can turn us outward toward others, and even for that, he awaits our free will and asking. Even the nervous but contemplative Mary, full of piety and love of God, can hug *her* interests tightly to herself until, like a hot rock plucked from the fire and held in her hands to warm them, she eventually turns stone cold. A neurotic Martha, too, remains so for as long as it takes her to realize that no one—not she nor I nor you—can ever stand still. Either we turn outward from self to others or we cool.

My return to a life of stability, even after I made up my mind to pull out of the all-consuming mire of self-interest and self-pity, was not immediate and miraculous. For you don't turn temperaments on and off like spigots at the sink and it's unreal to expect to. But after the decision was made, I found myself on a completely new course. I could begin to fight off this thing once I knew exactly what had been tearing me and my family apart.

There *had* to be causes for my distress because, though I only thought of them now with envy, I remembered past times when I had been loved and happy. Even that I had sung and laughed with the children. What had happened?

I knew there had to be physical reasons, at least at first, but did they have to hang on so long? Was I working too hard? Sleeping too little? The Mary who loved Jesus greatly and the Martha who served him so well, after all, were *two* strong women! And here I was, impulsively trying to go both ways at once. As if it were a strange new truth, it dawned on me that *nobody* can do it all! I had to stop and search for one of the middle paths.

I discovered I'd been spending more time praying for a lightening of my burdens than for the strength to carry them. And in my new relief at what seemed the right track, I immediately expected miracles of myself—the very quickest way to self-defeat. And a sure way right back into my Marthaisms.

New habits should easily replace old mental habits now, I thought. But it wasn't so. For one thing, even a bad habit is a loved thing. The way mine persisted while I was trying to rout them out showed me how foolishly I had been clinging to prevailing emotions just because they were habitual.

By expecting too much of myself, I was reinforcing the bad habits I was trying to break. Lack of good judgment about rest was a major problem. Worry and rest can't reside in the same mind at the same time. Which did I want? Work and rest can't be produced by the same body at the same time. Which did I want? *Recreation*, I thought, *is a thing somebody else does, not something for the likes of me.*

The moment the idea formed in my mind, I flushed for very shame. Pride finds strange ways to worm itself into our lives, doesn't it? What false humility it is, to say I had no right to recreation but others did. Was I not a person, too, even when I didn't feel like one? I was one of God's children even when I felt deserted. Then why did I not need recreation as surely as any other mortal being?

It took a lot of warring with myself to learn that I should be as kind to myself as I'd been to Bill and our children before these weeks when I'd turned into such a witch. Bill often told me I was too hard on myself, but not until now had I been able to listen. We need love so *desperately* when we are the most unlovable! Bill, for the most part, had just looked helplessly on and, I learned later, prayed his heart out, for I rejected his overtures as often as not, then turned away and lashed myself for being curt and cutting to him. I knew I needed desperately to have some time alone, just for myself. Given that, surely I could manage the other busy hours. OK, now I knew what I needed and I set about re-arranging our schedule, for every family has one, even if, like ours, it's an elastic, hit-or-miss, nonschedule schedule.

Since the miscarriage I'd tried to nap when the little ones were down, but invariably that hour had turned into a fit of worries. *I'm not going to just keep letting it happen*, I promised myself.

The next day I put the kids to bed, then instead of heading for my own nap, I sat down and picked up the Bible and looked at it with new eyes. It had been a long time. Maybe it would help me pray. I'd almost forgotten how. How many weeks had it been since I'd last sat down without stewing over something I couldn't help anyway? I couldn't remember. I opened it to the New Testament because it was more familiar and might be easier going. Already at one-thirty in the afternoon I was weary, so I read very slowly, saying the words aloud so they could sink in, and slowly I relaxed beneath their spell, lingering on: "On the last day of the feast, the great day, Jesus stood up and proclaimed, 'If any one thirst, let him come to me and drink. He who believes in me, as the scripture has said, "Out of his heart shall flow rivers of living water" ' " (John 7:37–38).

Those moments were so *good* while they lasted! And the words returned again and again like a benediction through the day. But in less than fifteen minutes my "private" time was over. The two preschoolers began to scrap over a book one had smuggled into the bedroom and the spell was broken. But I did make a more gentle referee.

No, I did not automatically and right then turn into a balanced Mary-Martha, cured of my nerves, not even momentarily. When we try to renew old and forgotten friendships, we don't immediately swing into intimacy. It takes a while to come close to God, too, and I'd been too long turned away from him. Already I suspected that I wouldn't be so handicapped by my emotions if our Lord were already a guest of my quiet thoughts.

Days passed—and I persisted, and became aware that fifteen minutes a day in touch with God, especially when regular, generates more energy than a dozen naps. It was like turning the switch on a dynamo. Everything else slipped into gear, settled into proper order, and finally I was in step again with Bill and the kids, and our family began to hum with an amazing meshing of purposes.

No longer did the washer and dryer sit there staring me down in a purposely staged effort to wear me out. They were not monsters, but only machines that cleaned clothes. Youngsters who had been fighting now only squabbled occasionally and normally when their antics no longer produced the negative attention which had been all they'd received from me since the miscarriage. Bill began to walk into the house with a smile on his face instead of that wary look, and his kisses were no longer pecks, but real signs of the affection he was once more reassured that we shared.

It was uncanny how needless conflicts, resentments, and jealousies surfaced and, when openly seen, vanished. Maybe it wasn't so uncanny. Selfishness can't stand too close an inspection.

I knew I tired far more easily than reaxed women, but now I discovered I refreshed as totally under a new awakening awareness of our Lord's warm love. But irritability is not easily chased, and I had to sandwich in extra slots of time for tidbits of nearness with him. Surely, I reasoned, it was the daily meditations that were producing this miraculous rapport between me and the family, because I had not been able to do it alone.

I've come to the conclusion that the difference between those who eventually climb out of their instability and those who continue to flounder there is the difference between allowing a loving Father to heal them, and turning away and refusing his helping hand.

Slowly, slowly, like our baby who was now toddling but tripping over his toes, I relearned the "simple" lesson I had learned before. *Until I could accept myself fully*, until I could *like* myself, I would never be rid of the selfishness and self-pity that had been posing as accusations and slights from others.

Self-indictment, I learned through bitter experience, is a cutdown of *other* people, even if indirectly. When I let myself become easily hurt, it was because *I* had first assumed the other person consciously *wanted* to hurt me. But not only are few people that mean-minded, most are just too busy to waste time running around making trouble. The few who did no longer could get to me, because I had at last discovered *they could not unless I let them.* When I refused to give space in my thoughts to unpleasant interactions with others when they did occur, my own hurts disappeared as if I'd tossed them onto a scrap heap.

Some emotional women fall victim to scrupulosity, a sickness one should avoid like galloping consumption or the hives. For it is a negative assumption that the merciful God hears only what we say and not what we intend, and is a denial of his mercy. It's a sure sign of how barren is one's trust of him.

I had become scrupulous, too, but in a different way, for *my* emptiness of faith was visited upon our children with devastating effect. During this down period, I was on them like a witch at the least slight or imagined slipup. They couldn't comb their hair right, tuck in their shirttails correctly, or even put food into their mouths to suit me.

I was impossible. Even I knew it. And even while I knew it, I felt helpless to stop myself. I realized, too, that I was being as hard on myself as I was on the children. Yet as long as our family was in such a state of chaos, I could not begin to be kind to myself. My conscience blocked it. I was trapped until I let my moments with God turn me around. Only then could I see that self-imposed improvement had to come first, and it had to begin with the Christ within me, for without him I was truly nothing. I made a list of my faults:

> I hated routine.
>
> I was fidgety and lost my temper easily.
>
> I did things in bits and dashes, jumping like a grasshopper to first one thing then another.
>
> I was sensitive and easily hurt.
>
> I panicked under pressure, even the kind I only dreamed up.

I don't know when I realized that the entire list was askew. That the characteristics sounded like faults because of my own distorted way of looking at them. I tried to get an objective view of myself. I tried to imagine how Christ, in all of his love and mercy, would think of me, and the list became:

> I was the one others called on when something came up unexpectedly and it upset their schedules. I *liked* surprises.
>
> Yes, I had a temper with a short fuse, but I felt it so keenly it gave me a sympathy and understanding of others who tended to dive into hot water as easily as I which many others didn't have.
>
> I did things in spurts, but I *did* finish what I started out to do. I was the one others could depend on to finish a job when everyone else got bored and quit.
>
> I was extremely sensitive—not only to myself but to other people and I keenly appreciated their smallest kindnesses. And I took the pains to tell them so.

Yes, I easily panicked, but I was very impuslive, too, so I as easily
and quickly offered to do things for others that were far more
than I could pull off. Better an offering of too much, however,
than being carefully cautious lest I give too much, or not offering
at all. Wasn't it?

The difference between the two viewpoints, of course, was
how well the person looking at them *liked* me. And when I
saw that, the panic, much of it, dissipated. I hadn't liked
myself for some time. Much of my failure clearly had only
been because I'd expected failure. I'd looked for problems
and expected disasters—mainly because I disliked being the
kind of person I really was. Obviously the difference in how
well I was growing as a person lay in whether *I* was thinking
of myself, of whether a forgiving and understanding God
was thinking of me.

Right there I sat, amazed, and wondered how long it had
been since I had treated my family with the love and mercy
which Chirst would have used. When and how and where
had I lost the desire to do his will instead of my own?

Self-pity, God help me, was the lingering habit that had
led me down such a dumb path. For no Christian mother can
get anywhere, soulwise, until the very tailored-to-fit pattern
of her life is stitched at every seam to the will of its Designer.
The garment we wear—our free will—must be pulled and
stretched and firmly stitched to form the perfect garment of
God's will, too, or we are slipping backward. Only as we
conform to his will can we become both the Martha mother,
responsible to her own and her family's physical needs, and
the Mary mother, acutely sensitive to her own and her family's spiritual needs.

Effort doesn't seem to count in all of this. If you are fidgety
and temperamental, fly off the handle at the slightest pro-
vocation, no matter how hard you—alone—try to calm
yourself, the whole attempt will continue to fizzle like a wool

suit in a hot dryer. For alone none of us can follow God's plan to be alive and loving. Only by tucking our will into his can we turn even *this* yoke of "nerves" until it fits the neat and useful garment of his will. Never will we find our heavenly Father forcing his will on us.

Therefore the busy Martha who says she has "no time to commune with God, not even for minutes a day" can go her way. But she does, I notice, take an hour a day for the morning coffee klatsch. Some haven't time for weekday prayers, but spend half an hour hesitating over which piece of fabric to choose for this dress or that pantsuit. Many have no time for spiritual reading, yet think nothing of regular luncheons with friends. Their excuses, as mine were, are often only Marthaisms, shortsighted ways of cheating ourselves of the spiritual growth that is ours for the making.

There is not a thing in the world wrong with coffee klatsches, the joy of shopping, or luncheons with friends. They are wonderful examples of how we manage to do exactly what we want to do most.

The world can be as beautiful or as gloomy as we choose to see it, for the Hand of God is always here to help us when we ask, to draw out the shape, the design of our lives. Christ did not say, "Come, lift up your cross like a feather and follow me." God always has known the kind of person you and I were to become. He made women, even the overemotional ones, *anyway*. He knew the small task for another would be a gigantic hurdle for the neurotic. He knew others would remain calm and busy and accomplish heroic things while those tangled in the web of overemotion worried and worried and tried and failed and failed.

But surely he only expects what each of us can give! From the impulsive Mary mother he expects the love of a Magdalene, the one who could not constrain her natural impulses until she found in Christ an understanding forgiveness that made her realize her own true worth. Did he not say,

"Therefore I tell you, her sins, which are many, are forgiven, for she loved much; but he who is forgiven little, loves little" (Luke 7:47)?

On the other hand, from the worrying, stewing Martha mother, our Lord only asks that she be less anxious. Did he not love Martha enough to raise her brother Lazarus from the dead?

The Mary-Martha balance as a goal is a very effective means of calming down nervous dispositions and dissolving guilt feelings about the negative provided we don't make of the improvement process a desperate measure. If we do, we defeat ourselves again. It does no good to wail, "Why me?"

It is far better, more beautiful and true to say instead, "God made me the way I am now, at this moment. Of course he always wants me to do better, but he loves me *for myself* while doing it."

Once I got that through my reluctant head, I was able to look at my life and myself as gently and lovingly as he does. Each characteristic can become a good quality because it *is* a good quality. It's our faulty use of it that goes awry sometimes, and a better Mary-Martha balance can set us straight again.

Like the Magdalene, I was born impulsive, and when I get nervous and easily upset, I spit out sarcastic words. Yet disliking that impulsiveness is a waste of energy. It isn't the impulsiveness that is the culprit, but my own lack of control of it. Continuously God offers comfort, love, and understanding; and my strengths are always in direct ratio to my closeness with God. To my Mary-Martha balance.

With that balance I can see the sharp and vibrant colors of an evening sky and feel the deep wonder of a little child's "Oh!" I can sense the exquisite beauty in the world so deeply that I *know* it comes from the good God.

No matter what the latest opinion is, whether a mother is happy where she is or not does *not* depend on the number of her children, be they one or three or thirteen. Because *situation* is seldom the real culprit. Maybe you're a Martha who hasn't learned, like Mary, to lean enough on our Lord. Where you are today is his doing, too, after all.

Can the nervous mother be a good influence on her children *right now*, in her present state? Of course, if she does everything she can to love them and to make sure they understand they're loved. Children have to learn compassion and beauty and concern for others. Right? Have we not seen more than enough of the children who grow up with a hard, unconcerned, callous attitude toward others? The "hands off" kids who let others beat up the small and helpless while they stand by?

Children have an immense capacity for understanding when mothers level with them. Once they understand that you're not feeling well today but that things will be better tomorrow, many tidal waves turn to little ripples in the home. Meanwhile, you're a mother who makes a fuss, and when it's over them, children can adjust to that too. It's only good sense for a mother to control her hysteria, because it scares youngsters, but concern and kisses for a skinned knee, warm hugs when you can think of no other way to get through, makes them feel warm and loved—*because they are.* And they are reassured by a mother who shows them she, too, knows how it feels to hurt.

There will probably always be times in my life when my personality will get in the way of what I'm doing. When it will get askew. When the pattern of my character, that tailored dress made according to God's will, will become tight and uncomfortable. So is that the dress's fault? Or the Martha within me who is allowing herself to go to pot? And when I don't control myself—it takes effort—I start to tear out a few stitches.

Any of us can occasionally pull a hem and the world purrs right on. We are not monsters, but neither will our least tizzy destroy our family *or* our civilization. I have my moments, even yet, when I feel, like Chicken Little, that the sky is falling. But most dreaded disasters are such only because I keep looking through the very narrow telescope of my own life—and through the wrong end at that.

All of the foregoing presumes, of course, that our nerves are produced by physical cycles or short-term results from some trauma each of us goes through at one time or another. But undoubtedly real and ugly despair can descend, too, and with or without warning. A woman this deeply troubled needs a physician as well as a priest or minister, and there's no use denying that such emotional conditions exist. The brain is a delicate instrument and we dare not take our own lack of capacity too lightly—so long as we don't renege, either, on our strengths. The mind being the complex thing it is, a woman in a state of despair from which she can't extricate herself should not, cannot, rest until she seeks help from qualified authorities.

Some people call despair a sin, a turning away from God. But only the mother who had experienced it knows how very fine is the line between her turning away from God—and her longing for him, *but feeling he has turned away from her.* Did not Christ, suffering on the cross, cry out in agony, "My God, my God, why hast thou forsaken me?" (Mark 15:34).

His was an agony of despair, too, if only to fulfill the prophesies. But the Father was standing by, waiting for his work of sacrifice for this world, for you and me, to be completed before releasing even his own Son.

But most periods of overemotionalism *can* be overcome, difficult though it is to forget that most interesting of people—oneself. When I have been the most guilt-ridden, it was because I was thinking too much *about* myself and not enough *of* myself. Once I returned to Christ, I no longer needed hesitate to follow my impulses for they were now colored with his goodness. Restraint is for petty flaws.

I spent many hours meditating thoughtfully on the Christ who strained under a cross so heavy he couldn't drag it alone. So that I—and you—need never be alone again. His cross made him fall, too, but he staggered to his feet only to fall again, the weight pressing his face into the stones and dirt. But he tottered to his feet once more only to fall a third time.

Meditations on his passion pulled many of my personal and selfish demands into perspective. Who are we mortal women—you and I—to bewail and dislike the nervous personality that causes *us* to stagger and fall and fall and fall, only to rise again with the same weakness ebbing and flowing within us? How can we hesitate to place our lives into the keeping of a Lord who stumbled even as we stumble?

In a way, we are peculiarly blessed. By our very natures, we are forced into a constant need of the Christ who also looked with such love upon the reluctant Simon of Cyrene, who had to be forced to help Jesus carry the cross too heavy to bear alone.

No one understands you and me and our faltering weaknesses better. This weakened one is the Christ who lives within us and has chosen *us* to be the earthly expressions of his love. He is willing to lighten our crosses if we let him, just as he let another lift his 2,000 years ago.

For you and I—the nervous mothers—cannot walk alone. Nor can the modern Martha who attempts two full-time jobs, one outside of the home, the other waiting to absorb her totally when that is done.

We cannot permit *anything* to absorb us totally except our Lord. For he alone shows us the guiltless way to a Mary-Martha balance. When to say no, when to say yes, without losing sight of him who is the spring of tranquillity that keeps us refreshed and steady.

15
Nearing the Goal

Admitting our faults can be the beginning of change, first within ourselves, then within our families, then outward to others, as we are brought to the reality again and again that no human being, mothers less than any, can find him/herself alone. Always when people are filled with personal enrichment, there follows the need to stretch outward to something, someone else. We are nearing our goal as Mary-Martha mothers when there is within us not only the tranquillity of soul we've longed for but much much more. The ability to see our families and others through the eyes of love and understanding no matter what our emotional reaction to them.

How recently have you been verbally attacked by someone and did not, at least mentally, write him/her off as mean and small-minded?

I'll never forget when I was a child of eight and I saw a picture in the paper of a well-known public figure. "I don't like him!" I said with the brash ignorance of a child. "He's mean. Look at his face."

My brother, seven years older and wiser, said, "Well, you're wrong. I've read a lot about him and he's been sick most of his life. It's pain that's put that look on his face and mouth. Years and years of pain. He's a very kind person, no matter how he looks."

Today's secular society contains many people as brash as I was, and many of them are octogenarians. These days one is actually treated as guilty until proven innocent and innocence is laughed at if found out.

You don't think so? How many chances does the victim of gossip get to redeem her reputation, even when the rumor is undeserved?

Love, on the other hand, is strange and healing and as unpredictable as quicksilver in your palm. It cannot be contained but keeps darting in and out, back and forth, making its own way, almost but not quite independent of who holds it. Christian love is even less our own doing because it is generated by the force of Christ's love with which we are entrusted. What are we doing with it? The barometer of spiritual health in family and in nation is plain for all to see by the measure of joy that rises within them.

Our beautiful nation "under God" has developed a curdled attitude about the goodness of humankind and only Christians can bring about its sorely needed change. We individual citizens, outraged and feeling betrayed by our leaders, have become like so many toenails with too much pressure put upon them—irritated, demanding, and ingrown.

Still, situations don't change themselves. People change them. I believe Christian mothers, Mary-Martha mothers, have it in their busy hands to change the world, because all of loving begins in the home. Loving in Christ's way means evaluating, not jumping to wrong conclusions, as I've so often been guilty of doing when I've failed to listen or because I wasn't sensitive enough to the needs of those around me.

When one of our babies was only nine months old, I learned how damaging to another rash judgment can be.

Larry had developed a raucous, demanding cry that got to me. I checked him to see if there were open pins, wet diaper, anything wrong, and found nothing. He had recently eaten but was not colicky. Why, then, did he act that way? His scream sounded just plain ornery to me. I assumed that's what it was and was impatient and uncomforting.

Three hours later I discovered the trouble when his screams crescendoed enough for me to realize them for the cries of pain they were. When I took him to the doctor, I found he had an infected ear. You can imagine how horrible I felt over my lack of understanding and impatience with such a tiny person.

You would think I'd have gone on, then, to become sweet and loving to the children whenever they sounded as if they needed something. And I did try—for a time.

Then I slid backward. At ten-thirty one morning Larry and Brian, three and two by then, began to fight and about the only thing I did right was to separate them, which didn't stop their "orneriness." The moment I went back to bed-making they were at it again.

It was an awful day and many more equally awful days happened before I got wise. The miracle of wisdom occurred the day I felt extra energetic and happened to make some graham-cracker cookies. You know, the kind with powdered sugar frosting to weld them together? By the time I'd finished making them, *again* Larry was shoving Brian, Peggy was caught in the middle and screaming, and even the baby had fallen backwards into his playpen, the loosened bars torn out and flying in his flailing fists.

I poured milk, offered them all cookies, and within minutes the house was peaceful. It was such a change a moron could have drawn the correct conclusion. *They had only been hungry!*

On this I didn't slip again. After that, when everything else was ruled out, I tried a snack and it invariably ironed out the troubles (I did *not* set up a system of rewarding with food that is a sure way to lead the child later into obesity, either. Looking back, I sometimes wonder how I avoided that one.) Actually, I've come to understand that sometimes their need in midmorning is as much a need for mom's attention as it is for something to put into their stomachs.

It doesn't pay to cry over errors we should learn from and forget. But if we want to teach the world to love again, we'll have to average better than I did on our kids' "orneriness." The only way we can be sure we're doing God's will is to put ourselves in his hands and let him push us in the paths he's already chosen for us.

Though the field of operation for today's Christian mother may well be contacts through a job outside her home or the limelight of public life, for most of us it will be within our homes and neighborhoods and so close to just family living that we are not aware of our tremendous value as witnesses for Christ. For teaching the world to love is as vital in the tiniest of kindnesses as it is in "important" work the world applauds.

It's simple to begin, and exciting because, when you join hands with God, your life begins to take unusual and unexpected but vitally rewarding paths. From each Christian mother flows a power as great as the universe and as practical as the here and now. It's wrapped in love and a kind word. But it takes a Mary-Martha balance to activate this power that lies within us, waiting to be turned on. As we near the goal, suddenly even impossible things become possible—and joy-filled—and it happens almost without our realizing it.

We find we're no longer on the negative path of self-recrimination and needless guilt. The closer we come to reaching our Mary-Martha balance, the more positive and outgoing our lives become. For it's not just our own child or children who need us, but every single person with whom we come into contact. They need to see in us this balance that holds us steady and serene as we allow the active force of Christ's love to do its work.

It's always deceptively easy to love all of humanity—but frighteningly difficult to love those who turn us off. Years ago we were living in a close-knit neighborhood where I knew and enjoyed all but one of ten young mothers. We were self-righteously outraged when, at seven every morning after her husband went to work, this woman turned her four children, whose ages ranged from four to ten, out onto the front porch, tossed their clothes out after them if they were half-dressed as they often were even in cold weather, and locked the door, pulled down the blinds, and kept them out until seven that night just before her husband returned.

I, as well as the others, was furious at what seemed her total unconcern and I still don't know why none of us called the authorities. At lunch and dinner times those four children would arrive at one or another of our houses, press their noses flat against the screen in the summer and the window when the door was closed, and stand there sniffing with hunger.

I didn't resent cooking for and feeding the children when they came to our house. I was too busy being angry with their neglectful mother. But I was wrong!

A full twenty years later I met the "negligent" mother whom I hadn't seen since we'd moved from the neighborhood, and with a very surface concern, I asked, "How are you these days?"

"You wouldn't *believe* how much better I feel now than I used to!" she exclaimed. "Do you happen to remember how sick I was when you lived next door? The slightest noise was more than I could take and the early mornings were hideous. I just couldn't *bear* to face the day. Well, finally the doctors found out what was wrong. I had pernicious anemia. They haven't cured it, but it's under control now and it's made a whole new life for our family."

I felt my face flame at my un-Christian misjudgment of her. *Where had I been when she needed someone so badly? One of us should have helped her!*

It is very, very easy to leap to such false conclusions. A sour stomach makes one act cranky and mean in exactly the same way a sour disposition does, but how often do we react to the sufferer with the same turning away?

Our attitudes toward others is an infallible measure of how near to our balance we are drawing. It's simple to say God is love and I am a Christian. But how do I react when the cantankerous old man down the street glares at me when we meet? Have I reached out with a persistent enough smile to learn that he suffers constantly from bunions and sore feet? There isn't enough real caring going on in the world, especially for those we find unlovable. It's easy to love our friends, as Sacred Scripture tells us, but what about those we think of as enemies?

I'm not so naive as to suggest each of us immediately, and in the name of Christ, rush out and turn into the neighborhood busybody. But too often we say, "I am a child of God" or the more modern "I am one of the people of God." But do we really believe it? Do we really act as if we are? There are unhappy, undecided people seeking answers, needing love, wherever we go. What are you and I—the Christian mothers—doing to help them? To understand and listen to them?

The first time I asked myself these questions, I found my Christian loving average so low I was certain I'd *never* be of use to God inside *or* outside of our home. Like most Marthas who have not learned the value of letting God do the leading, I was seeking perfection in myself and in every detail *for itself alone,* just as today's modern Martha seeks it.

Yet perfection in woman most closely resembles her physical features—full and rounded, conceiving and developing, changing and adjusting, teaching others but most of all teaching herself. Doing good for God's sake and not for guilt or mortal fear. For our Lord is more merciful than just, more loving than critical. Loving him means meditating *and* acting, because he wants us to carry our share of the load. Only a Mary-Martha balance can bring about this happy state of perfection and help us to return to it when we wander.

The prevailing sense that our society is morally bankrupt has become a constant topic of coffee-cup chat. The second most common topic is most homemakers' feelings of worthlessness. Is there a link?

There was a lonely period in my life when we had four children, the oldest seven, and I was expecting our fifth. I could not keep our home uncluttered. All of us were well, but I felt useless and terribly down. The occupational hazard of mothers, I've since learned, because the real worth of our work doesn't surface for at least fifteen years, more often twenty or thirty.

I looked into the mirror, examined the fault-filled me, and decided I had to learn to like this woman or drive us both wild. So I wanted a piece of the action out in the world, did I? Well, what was stopping me? My eyes faltered before their image.

What *had* been stopping me? The same thing that prevents most mothers from reaching their Mary-Martha balance, their greatest potential for good. Any positive feelings I had going for me were blanketed by inhibitions and feelings of inadequacy. My kids were not big enough for me to even feel sure *they'd* turn out right. Hadn't I heard the apple doesn't fall far from the tree? Who was *I* to think I had anything to offer?

Now, with thirteen kids and twenty years later, I know I

missed endless opportunities along the way because I kept downgrading the nearest of God's creations—me. We cannot judge anyone—not even ourselves—and grow, either as persons or as children of God.

We can try to keep our apples neat and close to the tree, but our best is all we have. No one can do more, so why get into a tizzy over it? Tizzies are as crippling as idle gossip and they're both too common.

It's deceptively easy to love all of humanity—and next to impossible to love the college son or daughter who has just announced he/she is throwing over the teachings we thought we'd planted so solidly. Do we care enough to listen, to hear them out—and then to love them *no matter what they do*, as they pick and choose their way, *their own way*, to Christ?

One of our sons came home from college in his junior year and blithely announced, "Mom, I've decided to leave the Catholic Church." His gaze dropped to his fumbling hands while Bill and I gasped in unison and in shock. I still don't know why I was not shouting the disappointment in him that made my head pound and my ears hurt. "I've found another church. One that has the *real* truth."

"But—but—how *could* you after all we—."

"Will you let me finish?" That was when it got through to me that his was a cry of anguish. A cry that we love him *and let him go* to do what he, at twenty-one, had decided he must do. I gulped, nodded, and glanced at Bill's tensed white knuckles. "I have to do what I think is right!" Our son's eyes blazed up into mine and the statement was a demand. "I *know* how you and dad feel! I *know* what you believe—."

Lives there a parent who has not wailed as I did then, "No! You *don't* know how we feel! *You couldn't possibly know!* What have we done that's so wrong? Why are you leaving the church I looked for so long and hard? The church I've been so sure of?"

The absurdity of my equating his needs so totally with my

own made even me stop right there. And our son was too charitable to correct me. "Mom," he said gently, "I want to spend my life serving Jesus Christ."

"What in the hell do you think *we've* been doing all these years?" Bill exploded at last.

His son offered him a lopsided grin and then all of us broke into hysterical giggles that broke some of the tension. Each of us was stumbling in the dark. "I know you've done what you think is best," he continued. "But don't you see? I have to follow *my* conscience too? What's so wrong about following Jesus?"

My tears were overflowing by now, but there was only one sensible answer. "Nothing. Nothing at all. It's what Dad and I have always prayed for."

And it was true. For we cannot live our own lives through our children. Their identities are theirs, not ours, even in such sensitive areas as religion.

The Christian mother who strives for a Mary-Martha balance is nearing her goal when she sees the loneliness today's young people feel as they take their first giant steps away and into the unknown, no matter what mistakes they make—and she loves them anyway. We cannot do their living for them. And sometimes we need to know how hard it is for them and others to be on the receiving end of love.

That lesson, too, I learned through mixed feelings as I experienced the receiving of love well intended but difficult to accept. When I came home from an extended stay in the hospital after our eleventh baby was born, women from our church came over the very next morning, mops and cleaning cloths in hand and ready to do my work for me until I was on my feet again. At first I felt awkward, then guilty, as two cleaned and cooked, while others took preschoolers for the day and returned them in the evening. Yet their marvelous offering of self, so concretely shown in physical effort, gave me a badly needed boost in learning how to love others and at the same time how to receive it. For being on the taking end is never as easy as it seems to the giver.

We're nearing our goal when we realize there *are* two sides to the helping of others. When we open our hearts to the Holy Spirit, unbelievable things can happen, even to the most unlikely of us. When we look around at the lonely, the unloved, the worried, the ill, all we need do is represent our Lord with a quick smile, a moment's time, and always with a gentle word. We don't have to be psychiatrists or social workers to listen to people. To be aware. Too often mothers, especially, hesitate to speak up because they feel unprepared and inadequate.

Only—Christian mothers *can* return the weary world to God. Mary-Martha mothers, whose children have taught them sensitivity to others, are therefore uniquely able to sense trouble when someone needs a friend. They are women into whose lives the Holy Spirit moves automatically with the little ones. We need only follow where it leads. We *can* teach love into the next generation. The tiny fists that curl around our hearts show us very early the value of being there with a smile, a word, a soft touch.

That we feel inadequate is unimportant. *Who was ever adequate* to represent Christ to others? Moses questioned God and yet he was told to lead the Jews. The Jews were led by God from slavery, but they forgot him and built a golden calf to worship instead—and yet he forgave them. Peter denied Jesus three times and still became the rock upon which Christianity was built. Like each of them, we, too, are weak as all mortals are weak unless we make time to be still and alone to seek our God.

With practice, our meditations lead us on to contemplation where we can feel the vacuum of our minds as they are emptied of today's worldliness. The waiting, the holding perfectly still and waiting—and finally the rushing back of the true inner self we had momentarily lost.

The renewed Mary-Martha thus is made once again into a whole and balanced person, round and complete as if there had never been a clock for her rule, as if there had never been children and husband picking and pulling little pieces of her away. In these odd moments we have found the spiritual grace that enables us to go forward as we were meant to do, with a tilt to our heads and a lift to our hearts which means we are walking with God and bringing our families with us.

Little by little these silences that light our way as we near our goal build up into an ocean of spiritual nourishment whose very tides break over into the lives of those around us. When we are filled with peace we not only desire, but see and feel, the active force of love that reaches more than anything else to help others to know that they are, also, as loved.

It is easy to speak of God as having always been. Difficult to the point of impossibility to perceive completely with our finite minds, how his eternal being continually provides us with such eternal help and strength if we will but use them.

It is our obligation and richest privilege as mothers to give of ourselves. But it is patently clear, too, that we must therefore make provisions for restocking our strength, our character, our spiritual self. The mother who has depleted herself of God's love is tragic. She it is who runs from neighbor to neighbor and friend to friend, and forgets the friend of all humankind.

What did she do with the half hour last night when she was too troubled to sleep? If she'd stopped to think, she might have realized that restlessness and nameless tensions are but a soul crying for its God.

The most important time in a mother's life is the time she spends alone—although it's hard to realize it until it is practiced. There are vast reserves that may be tapped only when one is alone, though sometimes mothers must settle for being alone in spirit. The creative person knows the value of aloneness. So does the artist for whom quiet precedes the creative rush. The beauty of the musician's symphony is directly related to the solitude of creation. Like them, every mother is a creative person whose very creativity will drain away unless she seeks help that is out of this world and she finds such help through a Mary-Martha balance.

Time alone awaits her as close as her church. Here precious holy hours can be hers before the tabernacle whenever she can arrange it and chooses to make them. Here she can turn almost completely to a Mary for a short, sweet while— one tranquil hour with Jesus.

Another source of strength, and easy because we return to it at least weekly, is community worship with its attendant graces.

But easiest and closest *and most effective* are the times in our homes when we work as we pray with one effort, offering each day to God. We make of our homes a shrine when we find there, and return to it daily, our own still nucleus that is oneness with God. The Christian mother sometimes fails to see her nucleus, her real inner being as it exists in the love she shares with husband, children, and community. Home life is so basic and so *everyday* that it's easy to forget how actively our Lord's love watches over us.

The day that stands alone as the happiest day of my life, not for my personal accomplishment, but for the love that returned to me so fully, is also the day I realized that Christian motherhood, the Mary-Martha balance, does not wait for heaven to bring us its rewards.

It began a little over a year ago when the chance I'd longed for all my life came along and I was almost afraid to take it. *Could* a fifty-four-year-old grandmother with a disabled husband and three teen-agers still at home keep up with them all and yet meet the high scholastic standards set by a four-year college?

That Fort Wright College of the Holy Names had accepted me as a full-time student at all was too good to be true. But their Non-Traditional Degree Program, a new concept in higher education, is tailored for older people like me; and I clutched at it with a desperation I'd not known I still harbored.

Even my husband couldn't believe it was real. "It's too good to be true," Bill said. "Are you sure it's a valid degree?"

Apprehensive myself, now, that it would slip away from me again, I rushed to the college, conveniently located in our city, to ask the vice-president for Finance and Development.

He chuckled at me. "Mrs. Hertz, I've taken this program to the state's Board of Accreditation. They've given it full approval. *There is no hitch!* Just because you're given some credits for proven professional and community work besides your completed courses doesn't mean you've not done this work. In many ways you've done far more than the average graduate."

But—but—."

"Look," he said earnestly. "we're not the only college doing this, you know; though we are the first in the Northwest. Your meeting with the Review Board satisfied the faculty that you meet the requirements they use for regular students. Now you only have the few remaining courses to finish." He grinned as relief must have shown on my face. "Any more questions?"

I shook my head. By the end of the year I could be *finished.* Unbelievable! I left his office high on opportunity.

No one can know what those first classes as a full-time student meant. I applied myself with frantic fervor, while Bill and the kids at home helped and they and two married daughters in town looked on and often were amused.

Sometimes I'd remember past years when friends, not always tactfully, suggested I'd been too involved in the community.

"It's bread cast upon the waters," was my standard reply.

"*Sure* it is." They shook their heads and offered some downbeat cliché such as "But watch it come back a soggy loaf."

Yet here it was, instead, *tenfold!*

Going to college was the more unreal for our having just had a tough eight years. Bill had been injured while seven of our children were still home. We gave up our motel business of nineteen years and I searched for work to supplement his meager Social Security disability checks, their amount geared for a maximum of three children.

But I was forty-eight and no matter how clean, neat, and attractive I made myself, employers repeatedly turned me down for either of two reasons, neatly skipping my business years because they had been our own and not salaried. Their reasons? "You're over-qualified for this job." (This kept me from the lower-paying ones.) "I know you're capable of the work, but you don't have the B.A. required." (This screened me out of the better-paying ones.)

I quit searching, finally, and stayed home to write and free-lance—and to pray. The children needed me close anyway. God must have his reasons.

In two years we managed a little better after I took a part-time job which lasted three years until I landed a full-time position which unfortunately dissipated in six months when our department was closed out. Again I looked for work and again the employers' two excuses surfaced. So I free-lanced once more to make use of the hours at home.

Then had come this unbelievable chance! A bachelor's degree in English and sociology was actually within reach. The months sped by as I completed the courses and at last commencement approached. Proudly I sent invitations to friends and family, thinking they'd be as pleased as I.

Vickie, our high school senior, said innocently that our teacher-daughter had called from Seattle. Bonnie couldn't come. She had field trips and last-minute exams.

"I was afraid of that," I said, and it never occurred to me that the real message might have been different.

A son phoned. "I'm sorry, Mom. We're both too swamped with work." His wife, too, was a teacher.

And I understood. Really. But somewhere inside of me

awakened a feeling I tried not to let in; yet I was helpless to keep it out. Disappointment that deepened as other letters and calls came.

"I'm working that weekend and can't get off," a son said. "Congratulations anyway, Mom."

"Dave has to work 'til midnight the night before," a daughter explained long-distance. "We'd be too dragged out driving all night with Kimmie and no sleep. Congratulations, though. I wish we could come."

Only they *had* come to weddings, and to Christmases, and with even less sleep. I tried not to feel hurt.

Another son's invitation was returned. He'd moved without informing me. I readdressed it in care of a daughter who would contact him, but never received an answer. Did he care—at all?

Ted, 450 miles away in a high-school seminary, called. "I can't make it, Mom. It's too far just for one weekend. But I'll be home for the summer in only a week."

"—just for one weekend" cut the deepest, though his reasoning, too, was logical. Life has often hurt me deeply when reasoning has been the most logical. Already I was missing our children more than I had since the first fledgling had left twenty-five years before. For *all* of them, except those in town and a son and his family in Seattle, notified me they could not make it—and all for excellent, logical, indisputable reasons.

Nobody but I seemed to realize that this priceless degree was the culmination of a dream of thirty-nine years. Even Bill was taking it casually.

At sixteen, I'd graduated from high school but with no money for college. I'd begun working to earn it, but met Bill and then love took first place.

Sometimes even afterward, I had dreamed of college, but as each of six sons and seven daughters were born, the dream receded further. Thirty-seven years passed and I was active in church, PTA, and community work. Occasionally I took college courses, requesting credits when they were optional, my submerged hope for higher education barely lingering, almost forgotten.

And now it had all come true. Commencement, *my commencement*, was two days away—and only a fraction of the family was bothering to attend. I felt terribly let down.

Even my identical twin, who'd promised to come the 400 miles to share "my day," called. "Joe [her husband] has developed complications and he's back in the hospital. I wish I could come. Be happy anyway."

"Sure. Thanks for calling. We'll pray for Joe." He'd just had heart-bypass surgery and I did understand. But her call put the final crimp in my beautiful day. We've always been very close.

Mentally I shook myself. *You're a big girl now. If you're adult enough to graduate from college, for Pete's sake, then be adult enough to know your accomplishments mean more to you than to anybody else. You're making too much of it. You have everybody's good wishes. What more do you want?*

I wanted *them*. But I had no choice. I lifted a trembling chin and had to make the best of it.

The night before the big day, I was provoked at the girls for being so reluctant to help clean house. "A few will be here, anyway," I said crossly.

We went to bed early so I could get a good night's sleep. I wanted to look rested tomorrow, and at fifty-four sleep helps. At fifty-four *anything* helps. But it was midnight before I dropped off. It seemed only minutes later the phone rang. I jumped to answer it. It was 4:00 A.M. "Hello," I yawned.

The voice of a friend across town said, "Jacky—the wife's badly upset. Can you come over and help her?"

"Sure. Be right there." They were distressed over a son's

illness and the mother needed someone with whom to talk it out.

It was 8:30 before I returned home, still tired but now too wide-awake and atingle over the day ahead for more sleep. So much for beauty sleep! Again I became piqued at the girls for not helping more with the house when children and grandchildren who lived close were coming. But worry over Sis's husband and the friend and her son kept me too preoccupied to really insist. I did what I could myself.

The sad note even overshadowed the morning baccalaureate service during which I realized how selfish I was being. The children *did* care. I was foolish to let personal pride bother me. So, the hours ahead would be an unreal dream I'd go through without fanfare. So be it. I lifted my chin again, telling myself I didn't *really* care. Being your own person is supposed to be all the fulfillment a woman needs.

Commencement would begin at 2:30. We ate a light lunch and were back at the college at 2:00. By now nervousness and excitement were chasing each other around inside of me until I was in a state. I put on my black gown with white velvet at the neck, saw that it made me look forty pounds heavier, but still grinned like a fool. The room was filled with students half my age, a few even as old as I, some, I knew, on the same program. We adjusted caps and added tassels bearing the magic numbers, "75."

A lump filled my throat as my perspective at long last righted itself and turned from myself to the children. Those in town had been wonderful. Peggy, though busy with a baby and two toddlers, as a graduation gift had made this white-and-gold polyester crepe summer suit I was wearing. She'd also done my short brown hair so that the mortarboard wouldn't crush it.

The teen-agers at home had made two kinds of potato salad, cinnamon rolls, and a Jello fruit salad, and had shopped for a boneless cooked ham "in case somebody drops in." Suddenly I remembered that this morning half of the cinnamon rolls, one potato salad, and the Jello seemed to have miraculously disappeared. I should have quizzed someone. They were eating too much.

My only real attempt to splurge had been the three bottles of pink champagne I'd bought. Well, whoever was here could celebrate, couldn't they?

Peggy had suggested I get six bottles and do it up right, but I'd grinned and replied, "Why? We want to celebrate, not get soused. There'll only be a few of us." It was the first liquor in the house since one bottle at Christmas when the children, all of them, had come.

Nostalgia all but swamped me again, but was cut short as we were asked to line up for the procession. My stomach shivered so deliciously I suddenly felt like skipping instead of marching. Would I forget to nod and bow toward the audience? I'd forgotten at rehearsal.

John, Peggy's husband, was in the vestibule ready to take pictures. Everything would be OK after all. I could see Bill looking around, Peggy and her children, and Lolly and her husband. It *was* a fine day, after all. With much more dignity than I felt, I took my place in the front row next to the platform which held the speaker and other dignitaries.

Only last year at the state university, a son who couldn't be here today had received his bachelor of science degree. But this, my own graduation, was different. Today was a long-nurtured dream made real.

In no time at all, I became idiotically pleased with myself. So I would not betray myself, I watched each of the speakers in turn and nearly burst trying not to sneak a glimpse of my family.

The self-control lasted less than ten minutes. My gaze meandered casually toward them—and sudden shock drenched me.

One of our sons who "just couldn't" come, was sitting beside Bill, a gratified smile on his face!

I looked away, then back again.

This time another son, the one who hadn't even answered, was there!

For one panicky moment I told myself the excitement and lack of sleep had been too much. That I was seeing things. I glanced over at them a third time and there was Ted! He was supposed to be 450 miles away! But his teasing face was split wide in a grin that in no time matched my own.

My dignity was shot. I heard little of the speaker's address or the awards given, for wondering how the boys had worked it out. When my name was called, I barely managed to walk primly to the platform to receive the precious diploma and shake hands; but I totally forgot to nod to the audience. Somehow I got back to my seat and the rest became a happy blur.

After the ceremonies, we filed out and at the doorway the rest of it happened. For there stood eleven daughters and sons, *all* of our kids but the two in California!

Completely overwhelmed, I hugged and kissed them and then somehow shed my cap and gown, tucked the souvenir tassel in my purse, and joined them for the brief reception. I was feeling very cherished but it was only the beginning.

The pictures John took will always mean more than *my* graduating from college at fifty-four. My own accomplishment, being my own person—for that was what it meant to me—had never for a moment separated me from the mom I'd always been. It was mom who graduated that day.

One daughter, Bobbi, who will receive her degree in psychology from the state university next year, expressed it for several. "I don't see why it's so special, Mom. But I figured if today was important to you, then it was important to me, too."

As she'd planned, we all met at Peggy's larger home afterward. "They stayed at our place last night," she chuckled. "See why I wanted extra champagne? Never mind. I got it."

I only realized how much they had done for me, even the

missing two, when a daughter handed me a tiny box. "Open it, Mom. It's from all of us."

Nestled inside on white satin was a gold pin with thirteen birthstones in it! More than once since so many had grown up I'd said I wanted a mother's ring, but always a kid's keen logic had intervened. "How could your finger hold up a ring that big? Thirteen is a lot of stones."

Now here it was in a brooch, their setting like the branches of a family tree."

"I love you guys," I blubbered.

"Peg and Vickie wrote asking everybody to chip in," someone said.

"Yeah. For the pin *and* for the feast," added another.

For by now the table was laden with a smorgasbord which included goblets of pink champagne, everything clearly showing long-range planning by young people who loved me. For here, too, were the missing salads and cinnamon rolls!

Ted had given his last five dollars and was cheerfully broke for his last week in school. Vickie and Robin, the youngest girls, besides cooking, had contributed baby-sitting money. Robin loves flowers and had also picked and arranged all over our house and Peg's—while not doing the housework—fragrant bouquets of lilacs because they're my favorite color. Our son-in-law's affection was implicit in their very presence in his home, for he is violently allergic to them—a fact I only discovered later.

But as great as Bill's and everyone's gifts and good wishes were, *it was the sharing of them that meant so much.* We have never been a demonstrative family, yet here was such a beautiful demonstration of how they cared that no other day of my life can ever match it.

Christian motherhood is a tremendous vocation and mine had taken long and insistent perseverence along a tightly stretched rope, as I tried to balance my own feeling with the saving strength of Jesus. I'm not at the end of it. Not at all. But now I can see where the other end is. I know at last that he *has* steadied me as I balanced, he's been near me, within me, lifting me, every wavering step of the way.

Because of our children and through our children, we Christian mothers are the bearers of the faith as truly as one tiny flame snuffs out the dark. By reading Sacred Scripture, by shared family prayer, by spiritual readings, by seeking Christ in community with others, by loving even before we are loved, but *most of all* by resting in our Lord, we find the nourishment and the force which flows on into the florescence of our soul—union with God.

A regular habit of spiritual exercises, of whatever length or depth, gradually helps us to reach our balance, the key. At that point we can see at last that the nucleus of our inner silence and peace is *not* what we thought we were seeking at all, but the balance of our Christian womanhood. Upon this balance depend the varying scales of our love and work as Christian wives and mothers—and as children, ourselves, of Almighty God.

Saint Paul's especially pointed caution to the Romans is equally valid for the modern woman who is making judgments for herself as never before: "I appeal to you therefore, brethren, by the mercies of God, to present your bodies as a living sacrifice, holy and acceptable to God, which is your spiritual worship. Do not be conformed to this world but be transformed by the renewal of your mind, that you may prove what is the will of God, what is good and acceptable and perfect" (Romans 12:1–2).

When we near the Mary-Martha balance, when we have found our inner selves, that transformation he speaks of, we shall find a treasure which has always been deep within ourselves. The vessel of our true being, a shrine diffused, exalted, and made full by the presence of the living God.